# North ̶C̶A̶B̶I̶N̶ CABIN COOKING

by Mary Brubacher
and
Margie Knoblauch

GARLIC PRESS
Excelsior, Minnesota

*We dedicate this book, with love and gratitude, to those who have generously shared their recipes with us. . . and to our families, the ultimate taste-testers.*

Published by Garlic Press
1465 Knob Hill Lane
Excelsior, MN  55331
612/474/3831

Edited by Vicki Stavig
Cover  photograph by Robert Sheppard
Book design by Sara Christensen

Printed in the United States of America

ISBN 0-934070-19-9

# Contents

# Introduction

"Going to the cabin" is a common phrase in the Upper Midwest. On weekends and holidays, we "cabin people," looking for a change of pace, flock to the North Country's lakes and forests. Too often, however, we work just as hard cooking at the cabin as we do at home.

We want to be proud of the food we serve, but we want to be "on vacation," too. The recipes we present here are intended to make time spent at the cabin enjoyable for everyone—including the cook. Many of these recipes can be made at home and taken to the cabin. Others are one-dish meals that can be prepared easily in the cabin kitchen. All are geared for the vacationer or weekend "cabin person."

We requested recipes from friends and relatives who have cabins, and from others who understand the need for more casual cooking while vacationing. We asked for recipes that are tasty and popular, can be made in advance and conveniently transported, are easy to prepare, and use ingredients that are readily available—even in small, out-of-the-way grocery stores and markets.

In gathering these recipes, we learned that most of us, when going to the cabin for a short time, prepare food at home and take it with us. By doing so, we can enjoy our leisure time and still have delicious "home-cooked" meals.

Organization is the key to having that leisure time. Plan menus and prepare food in advance, whenever possible. Measure and mix dry ingredients for a recipe at home, especially if that recipe requires spices or seasonings not stocked at the cabin. Put the mixture into a plastic bag or other container, and label it accordingly.

Sharing cooking responsibilities also helps ensure leisure time for everyone. When a cabin is being shared by two or more families, each family can be responsible for a meal. Having a

5

group of young people? Use a "caper chart," as the Scouts do, to assign meal-time tasks.

Planning ahead, sharing kitchen duties, and using the recipes presented here should greatly reduce the amount of time spent in cabin kitchens preparing meals.

To those who contributed these recipes, we extend a heartfelt "thank you." To the reader, we express our hopes that this cookbook helps "cabin cooks" everywhere have more time to relax and enjoy those golden days in the North Country.

# Appetizers & Snacks

# Curry Dip

**Great for a party or when just relaxing at home.**

**1 1/3 cups Hellmann's
  mayonnaise
2 tablespoons honey
2 tablespoons ketchup
2 tablespoons grated onion
Dash of salt
1 tablespoon lemon juice
7 drops Tabasco sauce
1 teaspoon curry powder**

Combine all of the ingredients. Serve with fresh vegetables. You can use cauliflower, green pepper, celery, carrots, tomatoes, mushrooms, etc.

# Nacho Dip

**An easy snack, or appetizer, for a group.**

**2 1-pound cans refried beans
1 large onion, chopped and
  sauteed
1 4-ounce can chopped
  green chilies, drained
1 11-ounce bottle mild taco
  sauce
1 pound shredded Cheddar
  cheese
1 pound shredded Monterey
  Jack cheese**

Layer ingredients in order listed in a 9-by-13-inch pan.

Bake at 325° for 25 minutes. Dip into it with nachos, crackers, etc.

# Baked Cheese Dip

### So simple to make, and so good.

1 cup mayonnaise (not low-
    calorie)
1 cup sharp Cheddar cheese,
    grated
1 medium onion, cut very
    fine, or grated

Mix all ingredients. Put in a shallow oven dish or 9-inch pie plate. For color, you may sprinkle with paprika or parsley.

Bake at 400° until brown, 15 to 20 minutes. Do not over-bake. Serve with crackers or fresh vegetables. Recipe may be doubled for a large group.

# Rye and Dip

### Make dip at home, and take it with you. Prepare bread at last minute.

1-pound loaf unsliced rye
    bread
2/3 cup sour cream
2/3 cup mayonnaise (not
    salad dressing)
1 teaspoon dill weed or
    dill seed
1 teaspoon Beau Monde
    seasoning
1 tablespoon onion flakes
1 tablespoon parsley

Cut oval or rectangular hole in top of bread. Remove this bread, and break into bite-sized chunks. Make dip out of remaining ingredients. Refrigerate overnight.

Fill loaf with dip, and sur-round with bread chunks for dipping. (You may want to double the dip recipe.)

## Dip for Raw Vegetables

2 cups sour cream (or 1 cup
    sour cream and 1 cup
    mayonnaise)
1 package Knorr's vegetable
    soup mix
1/4 teaspoon curry, optional

Combine ingredients.

Refrigerate for at least 1 hour
before serving with chips or
fresh vegetables.

## Chopped Vegetable Spread

**Great with Wheat Thins. If you have a food processor,
the chopping will be a snap!**

1 cup chopped celery
1 green pepper, chopped
1 small onion, chopped
1 large cucumber, chopped
1 package unflavored gelatin
2 cups mayonnaise
1 teaspoon salt

Drain juice from vegetables.
Mix gelatin with 1/4 cup cold
water. Add 1/4 cup boiling
water. Mix with mayonnaise
and salt. Mix into vegetables.
Chill.

## Salmon Spread

**Men really like this one.**

8 ounces cream cheese,
    softened
1 16-ounce can salmon (pink
    or red), drained, flaked
    and deboned
1 tablespoon lemon juice
1 tablespoon grated onion
1/4 teaspoon liquid smoke
1/4 teaspoon salt
Snipped parsley

Combine all ingredients, except parsley. Refrigerate for 8
hours.

Serve in small glass bowl or
make a "mound" on a plate.
Sprinkle with snipped parsley.
Serve with Kavli (Norwegian
flat bread) or plain crackers.

## Zucchini-Cheese Spread

4 small or 2 medium
   zucchini, peeled and
   shredded
1 tablespoon diced onion
3 cups grated cheese
   (Cheddar, Colby, etc.)
Salt and pepper to taste

In ovenproof dish (approximately 8-inches-by-5-inches) layer 1/2 of the zucchini, 1/2 of the onion, salt and pepper and 1/2 of the cheese. Repeat layering.

Bake, at 350°, only until cheese melts, about 8 minutes. Serve with crackers.

## Quick Shrimp Spread

8 ounces cream cheese,
   softened
1 bottle chili sauce
1 6-1/2-ounce can of tiny
   shrimp, drained

On a shallow dish, like a small platter, spread creamed cheese. Cover with chili sauce—you may not need an entire bottle. Put shrimp on top of this. Serve with crackers.

## Two Easy Cream Cheese Appetizers

1 package cream cheese,
   rolled in lemon pepper

1 package cream cheese,
   topped with peach
   chutney

Serve with crackers.

# Cheese Balls

**Great for camping. Do ahead and freeze.**

1 8-ounce package cream
   cheese, softened
1 small jar pimento, cut up
1 4-ounce package smokey
   flavored Cheddar
   cheese, shredded
1/2 cup butter or margarine,
   softened
1/2 teaspoon salt
Garlic salt
2 tablespoons minced onion
Worcestershire sauce
Chopped nuts or parsley

Mix all ingredients in an electric mixer. Form into 3 balls. Roll in chopped nuts or parsley. Place in refrigerator until firm. Wrap and freeze.

Serve with crackers.

# Hot Triscuit Hors D'oeuvres

**Good and easy.**

4 ounces shredded
   Mozzarella cheese
4 ounces Cheddar cheese,
   shredded
1/2 6-ounce can black
   olives, chopped
6 green onions (with tops),
   finely chopped
1/2 cup Hellmann's
   mayonnaise

Combine and mix all ingredients. Spread on Triscuits.

Bake at 375° for 7 minutes.

## Hot Dried Beef Appetizer

1 8-ounce package cream
   cheese
1/2 cup sour cream
3 tablespoons milk
1 2-1/2-ounce jar chipped
   beef
1/4 cup minced green
   pepper
1/2 teaspoon garlic salt
2 tablespoons horseradish
1/2 cup chopped nuts

Beat cheese, sour cream and milk with mixer until well-blended. Add remaining ingredients, except nuts. Pat into a buttered, 8-by-8-inch baking dish. Top with nuts.

Bake at 350° for 20 minutes. Serve with crackers. May be prepared ahead of time, and baked later.

## Howie's Dill Pickle Special

1 medium jar dill pickles
1 2-1/2-ounce jar dried beef
1 package cream cheese,
   either size, depending
   on how many servings
   you desire

Soften cream cheese. Dry pickles with paper towels. Spread slice of dried beef with cream cheese to the edge.

Roll dried beef around pickle, with cream cheese next to the pickle. Insert toothpicks through each pickle at 1/2-inch intervals. Slice the wrapped pickles into 1/2-inch pieces. Cover.

Refrigerate until serving time.

# Taco Dip Hors D'oeuvres

**It's a winner! Even those who are not Mexican food fans love it.**

**1 8-ounce package cream
   cheese, softened**
**1 8-ounce carton sour cream**
**1/8 teaspoon garlic salt**
**1/2 head lettuce, shredded**
**2/3 cup chopped onion**
**1/4 cup chopped green
   pepper**
**2 tomatoes, chopped**
**1 cup Cheddar cheese**
**2 teaspoons pitted black
   olives**
**Taco sauce**

Combine cream cheese, sour cream and garlic salt. Mix well. Spread on shallow plate. Place in refrigerator for 15 minutes.

Sprinkle lettuce, onion, green pepper and tomatoes over the cheese mixture. Sprinkle cheese and olives over entire mixture. Dot with taco sauce, just before serving. Serve with taco chips for dipping. Can be prepared early in the day.

# Mini-Pizza

**A snack or appetizer.**

**Ritz or Triscuit crackers**
**Slices of cheese singles,
   cut into 1/4s**
**Tomato sauce**
**Pepperoni slices**

Layer in order listed.

Bake at 350° for 3 to 5 minutes.

# Dill Squares

**Combine the butter mixture with cheese at home, and refrigerate until needed at your destination.**

1/4 pound (1/2 cup) butter, softened
1/4 teaspoon Tabasco sauce
1/4 teaspoon Worcestershire sauce
1/4 teaspoon onion powder
2 teaspoons dill weed
Dash of cayenne
1 5-ounce jar Old English cheese
1 loaf Pepperidge Farm very thin, white bread

Blend first 6 ingredients. Add cheese. Mix well. Spread slice of bread with the butter-cheese mixture. Put second slice of bread on top. Spread cheese mixture on top of this slice, also. Trim crusts from "sandwich," and cut each into 6 squares. *This must be cut before baking.* Place on cookie sheet.

Bake at 350° for 15 minutes, or until brown.

# North Country Seafood Cocktail

**This one will fool your relatives from the sea coast. It's a great way to use leftover cooked fish—sunnies, crappies, bluegills, northerns, or walleyes.**

Pre-cooked fish
Seafood cocktail sauce
Shredded lettuce (optional)
Lemon slices (optional)

Break fish into bite-sized pieces, removing skin and bones. Mix with cocktail sauce. Serve individually in a cup or small glass as an appetizer, or on shredded lettuce with lemon as a garnish.

## Bite-Sized Stuffies

### You will love this one.

1 loaf frozen bread dough,
    thawed
36 stuffed green olives,
    cubes of ham, cheese
    or shrimp
Butter

Thaw dough overnight in refrigerator. Cut thawed dough into 36 pieces with scissors. Shape each piece around meat, olive, cheese or shrimp. Seal well. Place on greased cookie sheet. Cover and let rise until puffy.

Bake at 400° for 10 to 12 minutes. Brush with plain or garlic butter.

May be prepared in the morning to be baked later in the day. Place on greased cookie sheet in refrigerator. Let rise at room temperature at least 1/2 hour before baking.

# Gorp

**A nutritious snack, easy to make. Packable and portable for the outdoor enthusiast.**

Raisins
Dry roasted peanuts
Sunflower seeds, shelled
Slivered almonds

Choose one of the
    following:
M&M's candies
Reese's peanut butter pieces
Carob chips
Chocolate chips

Mix equal parts of all ingredients. Store in covered container or plastic bag.

# Caramel Corn

2 bags Old Dutch Puffcorn
2 cups brown sugar
1 cup margarine
1/2 cup light corn syrup
1 teaspoon vanilla
Pinch of salt
1/2 teaspoon baking soda

Combine brown sugar, margarine, corn syrup, vanilla and salt in saucepan. Boil for 5 minutes, stirring often. Remove from heat and stir in baking soda. Pour over Puffcorn in a large roaster, and stir well.

Bake at 250° for 1 hour, stirring every 15 minutes. Cool on a cookie sheet or tin foil.

# Breads & Breakfasts

## Susie's Simple Beer Bread

3 cups self-rising flour
1 can of beer, at room
   temperature
4 tablespoons sugar

Combine ingredients. Mix well. Pour into well-greased bread pan.

Bake at 350° for 45 minutes. Makes great toast, too!

## Prairie Brown Bread

**A wonderful, hearty, quick bread that freezes well.**

4 cups whole wheat flour
1 1/3 cups all-purpose flour
1 quart buttermilk
2 cups brown sugar
4 teaspoons baking soda
1 teaspoon salt

Thoroughly mix all ingredients. Pour batter into greased bread pans. This will make 2 large, or 4 small, loaves.

Bake large loaves at 350° for 1 hour. Check small loaves after 40 minutes. Remove from pans to cool on rack.

## Strawberry Bread

### Freezes well.

3 cups flour
2 cups sugar
1 teaspoon baking soda
1 1/2 teaspoons cinnamon
1 teaspoon salt
1 3-ounce package straw-
    berry Jell-o
4 eggs, beaten
1 16-ounce package frozen
    strawberries, thawed
1 1/4 cups butter or
    margarine, softened
1 1/4 cups chopped walnuts

Sift dry ingredients, including Jell-o, into a large bowl. Make a "well" in this mixture. Mix other ingredients in a small bowl, then pour into "well," and stir by hand. Pour into greased and floured loaf pans.

Bake at 350° for about 1 hour, until inserted toothpick comes out clean. Makes 5 very small loaves (3-by-5-inch size). Can use larger pans, and bake accordingly.

## Banana Blueberry Bread

### Keeps in the refrigerator for weeks.

3 cups unsifted flour
1 1/2 cups sugar
4 teaspoons baking powder
1 teaspoon salt
1 1/2 cups quick-cooking
    oats
2/3 cup vegetable oil
4 eggs, slightly beaten
2 cups mashed bananas
2 cups fresh or frozen
    blueberries

Mix flour, sugar, baking powder and salt. Stir in oats. Add oil, eggs, bananas and blueberries, stirring just until mixed. Pour batter into 2 greased 8 1/2-by-4 1/2-inch loaf pans.

Bake at 350° for about 60 minutes. Let cool in pan for 10 minutes, then remove from pan to a wire rack. When cool, wrap and refrigerate for several hours before slicing.

# Monkey Bread

**The aroma of this bread will act as a magnet for anyone in your cabin, including the cook.**

**4  7 1/2-ounce tubes
    refrigerated buttermilk
    biscuits
1 cup sugar
1 teaspoon cinnamon
1 cup brown sugar
3/4 cup margarine**

Cut each biscuit into quarters. Mix sugar and cinnamon. Dip biscuit pieces into sugar mixture or shake in a plastic bag. Put pieces in a well-greased angel-food pan or bundt pan.

Melt brown sugar and margarine. Do not boil. Pour over pieces in cake pan.

Bake at 350° for about 30 minutes. Let cool for 10 minutes, then turn upside down on a plate. Tear off pieces, or cut into slices.

## Very Lemon Bread

**Freezes well.**

1/2 cup shortening
1 cup sugar
Grated rind of a lemon
2 eggs
1/2 cup milk
1 1/2 cups flour
1 teaspoon baking powder
3/4 teaspoon salt
1/4 cup sugar
Juice of 1 lemon

Cream shortening and sugar. Add lemon rind. Beat in eggs. Sift dry ingredients. Add alternately with milk to first mixture.

Bake in 9-by-5-inch loaf pan at 350° for 50 to 60 minutes. Remove from pan while warm.

Mix sugar and lemon juice. Spoon over the bread. Prick the top with a fork, so bread will absorb the juice.

## Blue Cheese Bread

1 loaf French bread, sliced
    about 1-inch thick
1/2 cup butter
1/4 cup blue cheese,
    crumbled
1/4 teaspoon salt
1/8 teaspoon pepper

Combine butter, cheese, salt and pepper. Spread on each slice of French bread. Wrap bread in foil.

Bake at 400° for 20 minutes. Serve hot.

## Swedish Hard Tack

**Similar to flat bread, but tastier, we believe. Serve it "for coffee," with salads, or just to eat anytime.**

**3/4 cup butter**
**1/2 cup sugar**
**2 cups cracked wheat**
    **(quick-cooking oatmeal**
    **may be substituted)**
**3 cups white flour**
**1 teaspoon salt**
**1 teaspoon baking soda**
**1 1/2 cups buttermilk**

Cream butter and sugar. Mix dry ingredients. Add to creamed mixture, alternating with buttermilk. Form into balls the size of small baseballs. Cover, and let "rest" for about 1 hour. Roll thin as for pie crust.

Bake on cookie sheets for 15 minutes at 375°. Watch closely near end of baking time—when it starts to brown, remove from oven. When cool, break into pieces, and store in airtight container.

## Whipped Cream Biscuits

**Only two ingredients in these quick, light biscuits!**

**1/2 pint whipping cream**
**1 1/4 cups self-rising flour**

Whip cream until it forms soft peaks. Add flour. Mix. Drop by tablespoonful onto ungreased cookie sheet.

Bake at 375° for about 10 minutes, or until light brown.

Makes 12 biscuits.

# Celery Loaf

**A unique way to fix bread.**

1-pound loaf unsliced, white
    bread
1/2 cup butter or margarine,
    softened
1 teaspoon celery seed
1/4 teaspoon salt
1/4 teaspoon paprika
Dash of cayenne pepper

Trim crusts from top, sides and ends of loaf. Mix remaining ingredients. Spread over top of loaf. Cut loaf at 1-inch intervals from the top almost to the bottom crust. Spread mixture sparingly over both sides of slits. Place on cookie sheet.

Bake at 400° for 15 to 18 minutes, or until golden brown. Before serving, cut loaf through to the bottom.

If you wish to make ahead of time, cover with wax paper and refrigerate until time to bake.

# Beer Muffins

**These muffins are quick and easy and have a certain pizzazz!**

2 cups Bisquick
2 tablespoons sugar
1 cup beer
4 ounces (about 1 cup)
    shredded Cheddar
    cheese (optional)

Mix all ingredients. Fill greased muffin cups 2/3 full of batter. Let stand at least 10 minutes.

Bake at 375° for 15 minutes.

Makes 12 muffins.

# Parmesan Toast

**This is especially good as an appetizer or served with salads.
Watch out...it's addictive.**

**1 loaf baguette French bread
(smaller in diameter
than regular French
bread)
1 pound butter, melted
8-ounce can Parmesan
cheese**

Slice French bread into
1/4-inch slices. Quickly dip
each side in melted butter,
then in Parmesan cheese.
Place in jelly roll pan.

Bake at 325°. After about 8
minutes, drain any unmelted
butter from pan, and turn
each slice over. Continue
baking for another 8 minutes.
Remove from pan and put on
paper toweling to absorb any
excess butter.

You may need slightly more
than 1 pound butter or 8
ounces of Parmesan, depending on the size of the bread
loaf. Store in airtight container. It freezes beautifully.

## Scandia Valley Skillet Biscuits

**2 tablespoons butter**
**1 cup buttermilk**
**1/4 teaspoon baking soda**
**1/2 teaspoon salt**
**1 3/4 cups flour**
**1 tablespoon baking powder**

Melt butter in 8-inch iron skillet. Remove excess butter, and set aside for later use. In a small bowl, stir soda into buttermilk. Combine dry ingredients in another bowl. Mix well. Add this to the buttermilk; stir only until moistened and mixed well.

Knead on floured board about 15 times. Press dough to 1-inch thickness. Cut with floured cutter. Place biscuits in skillet, and spoon remaining butter over top of biscuits.

Bake at 450° for 12 to 15 minutes, or until biscuits are medium brown. Serve hot.

Makes about 8 biscuits.

# Thumbprint Pastries

1 10-ounce can refrigerated
   big flaky biscuits
1/2 cup sugar
1 teaspoon cinnamon
1/4 cup butter or margarine,
   melted
Jam or preserves (jelly is
   too thin)

Combine sugar and cinnamon. Dip both sides of each biscuit into melted butter, then in sugar-cinnamon mixture. Make deep thumbprint in center of each roll. Fill with 1 teaspoon jam.

Bake in ungreased 9-by-13-inch pan, or jelly roll pan, at 375° for 15 to 20 minutes, or until golden brown.

Makes 10 pastries.

# Sour Cream Coffee Ring

**Freezes well.**

1/2 cup margarine or butter
1 cup sugar
2 eggs
1 cup sour cream
1 teaspoon vanilla
2 cups flour
1 teaspoon baking soda
1 teaspoon baking powder
1 teaspoon salt
1/4 cup brown sugar

*Topping:*
1/2 cup chopped nuts
1/2 cup brown sugar
2 teaspoons cinnamon

Cream margarine and sugar. Add eggs. Mix. Add remaining ingredients. Put half the batter into a greased 10-inch tube pan. Sprinkle with half the topping. Repeat.

Bake at 350° for 45 to 50 minutes.

# Swedish Kringler Coffee Cake

## Delicious.

1 cup flour
1/2 cup butter
1 - 2 tablespoons water

Mix flour, butter and water, as for pie crust. Press into a jelly roll pan (11-by-16-inch), or press into two 4-inch-wide strips the length of a cookie sheet (this choice would be baked on a cookie sheet).

1 cup water
1/2 cup butter
1 cup flour
3 eggs
1 teaspoon almond extract

Heat the water and butter to boiling. Remove from heat. Stir in flour, beating until smooth. Add the 3 eggs, 1 at a time, and beat until smooth after each one. Add almond extract. Spread over crust.

Bake at 375 ° for 45 minutes.

*Icing:*
1 cup powdered sugar, sifted
1 1/2 tablespoons cream
1 tablespoon butter,
    softened
2 teaspoons almond extract

Beat icing ingredients. Spread on top of cake. Sprinkle with sliced almonds.

# Banana Muffins

**These moist muffins are worth the effort! Make in advance, and take them along. They freeze well.**

2 cups sugar
1/2 cup shortening
2 tablespoons salad oil
2 cups mashed bananas
3 eggs
2 1/4 cups cake flour
2 1/2 teaspoons baking soda
2 1/2 teaspoons baking
   powder
3/4 teaspoon salt
3/4 teaspoon vanilla
1 1/2 teaspoons lemon juice
1 cup buttermilk

Cream sugar, shortening and salad oil. Add bananas, and cream well. Add eggs, and mix well. Combine dry ingredients, and add to first mixture. Add vanilla and lemon juice. Mix well at low speed. Gradually add buttermilk, until smooth. Mix at medium speed for 3 minutes. Put into greased or paper-lined muffin pans.

Bake at 380° for 20 to 22 minutes.

Makes about 2 dozen muffins.

# Big Pine French Toast

2 cups milk
4 eggs, well-beaten
1/2 teaspoon salt
2 teaspoons cinnamon
   (optional)

Mix all ingredients. Dip bread into mixture until well-coated.

Fry on oiled griddle or fry pan until golden brown.

Makes 24.

# Blueberry Muffins

### Freezes well.

1/2 cup margarine
1 1/2 cups sugar
2 eggs
1/2 cup milk
1/2 teaspoon salt
2 teaspoons baking powder
2 cups flour
2 1/2 cups (1 pint) frozen
  or fresh blueberries

Using a spoon, mix all ingredients, except blueberries. (Do not use a mixer.) Fold blueberries into batter. Line muffin tins with paper cups. Fill to top of paper liner. Sprinkle each muffin with a teaspoon of sugar.

Bake at 375° for 25 to 30 minutes.

Makes 16 muffins.

# Breakfast Muffins

1/3 cup margarine
1/2 cup sugar
1 egg
1 1/2 cups flour
1 1/2 teaspoons baking
  powder
1/2 teaspoon salt
1/4 teaspoon nutmeg
1/2 cup milk
1/2 cup sugar
1 teaspoon cinnamon
1/2 cup margarine, melted

Combine and mix margarine, sugar and egg. In another bowl, combine flour, baking powder, salt and nutmeg. Add dry mixture, alternately with milk, to first mixture. Fill greased muffin cups 2/3 full.

Bake at 350° for 20 to 25 minutes.

Mix sugar and cinnamon. Immediately after baking, roll hot muffins in melted butter, then in sugar. Serve hot. Makes 12 muffins.

# Bran Muffins

**Batter can be stored in refrigerator up to 6 weeks. A good fiber food to have on hand for those who love to drop in!**

1 15-ounce package Raisin
  Bran
5 cups flour
5 teaspoons soda
2 teaspoons salt
3 cups sugar
1/2 cup vegetable oil
1/2 cup butter, melted
1 quart buttermilk, at room
  temperature
4 eggs, lightly beaten
1 cup nuts, chopped
1 cup raisins or dates

Melt butter. Let cool. In a 4-quart bowl, combine cereal, flour, soda, salt and sugar. Mix oil, butter, buttermilk, eggs, nuts and raisins. Stir into dry ingredients. Cover lightly. Store in refrigerator. Use as needed. Fill greased muffin cups 2/3 full with batter.

Bake at 350° for 20 minutes.

Makes 6 dozen muffins.

# Pumpkin Raisin Muffins

**Freezes very well.**

1 30-ounce can pumpkin
  pie mix
2 16.1-ounce packages nut
  bread mix
1 egg, beaten
1 cup raisins
2 tablespoons sugar
1 teaspoon cinnamon

Heat oven to 375°. Combine pumpkin pie mix, nut bread mix and egg. Mix only until bread mix is moistened. Stir in raisins. Fill greased muffin cups or paper muffin cups 2/3 full of batter. Combine sugar and cinnamon. Sprinkle on top of muffins.

Bake 15 to 20 minutes, or until golden brown.
Makes 30 muffins.

## Toasty Nut Granola

**This is a popular, nutritious and filling breakfast cereal for the late-rising college crowd. It tides them over until noon without messing up the kitchen!**

**6 cups oatmeal, uncooked**
**1/2 cup brown sugar**
**3/4 cup wheat germ**
**1/2 cup coconut**
**1/3 cup sesame seeds**
**1 cup chopped nuts**
**1/2 cup vegetable oil**
**1/3 cup honey**
**1 1/2 teaspoons vanilla**

Heat oatmeal at 350° in ungreased 9-by-13-inch pan, for 10 minutes. Mix brown sugar, wheat germ, coconut, sesame seeds and chopped nuts into heated oatmeal.

Combine vegetable oil, honey and vanilla. Add to first mixture, coating dry ingredients. Divide mixture into two equal parts, putting each in a 9-by-13-inch pan (or bake one pan at a time).

Bake for 20 minutes, stirring often to brown evenly. Cool. Store in tightly covered container. Add raisins, if desired.

Serve with milk and fresh fruit, if desired. This may also be used as a topping for vanilla ice cream.

## Apple-Oatmeal Baked Breakfast

**A delicious way to "take the chill off" on a crisp morning!**

2 cups milk
2 tablespoons brown sugar
1 tablespoon butter
1/4 teaspoon salt
1/4 teaspoon cinnamon
1 cup rolled oats
1 cup apples, peeled and
   diced
1/2 cup raisins

Combine milk, brown sugar, butter, salt and cinnamon in a pan. Scald. Add oats, apples and raisins. Heat until bubbles appear at edge of saucepan. Put into greased 1 1/2-quart casserole.

Bake at 350° for 30 minutes. After 15 minutes of baking, stir in 1 tablespoon of brown sugar. Serve with milk or cream.

Serves 4 to 6.

## Puffy French Toast

1 cup flour, sifted
1 1/2 teaspoons sugar
1 1/2 teaspoons baking
   powder
1/2 teaspoon salt
1/4 teaspoon cinnamon
1 cup milk
1 egg, beaten
8 slices white bread
Fat for deep frying

Sift dry ingredients. Blend milk and egg. Add to flour mixture. Beat until smooth. Dip bread slices into batter, turning to coat both sides evenly.

Fry in preheated deep fat (375°) until golden brown, about 2 minutes on each side. Drain. Serve hot.

Makes 8 slices.

## Frozen Orange French Toast

2 eggs
1 cup orange juice
1 tablespoon sugar
1/4 teaspoon salt
12 slices French bread
6 tablespoons butter or
    margarine

Advance preparation: Beat first 4 ingredients. Dip bread into egg mixture, coating both sides. Place bread on baking sheets. Freeze until firm. Wrap. Return to freezer.

Before serving: Place bread slices in well-buttered, shallow baking pan. Melt butter, and drizzle over bread.

Bake in 500° oven for 5 minutes. Turn over, and bake about 5 minutes more. Serve with syrup and butter, if desired.

Serves 6.

## Hootenanny Pancakes

1/2 cup margarine or butter
6 eggs
1 cup milk
1 cup flour
1/2 teaspoon salt

Melt butter in 9-by-13-inch glass pan in 425° oven. Beat eggs and milk. Add flour and salt. Do not overbeat. Pour into pan.

Bake for 25 to 30 minutes. Serve with syrup, jam, jelly, powdered sugar, cinnamon sugar or thinly sliced apples. Serves 6.

# Make-Ahead Pancake Mix

## Store in a covered container. Handy!

10 cups flour
2 cups powdered milk
6 tablespoons baking
   powder
1 1/2 tablespoons salt
1 1/2 teaspoons cream of
   tartar
1/4 cup sugar
2 cups shortening

*Pancakes for 4:*
1 cup milk
1 egg
1 1/2 cups pancake mix

Sift dry ingredients 3 times. Cut shortening into dry mixture. Store in covered container.

Beat milk and egg. Add mix.

Bake on a hot griddle.

# Crisp Waffles

**This recipe is especially good for thick waffles similar to those cooked in a Belgian Waffler.**

2 eggs, separated
1 cup flour
1 cup milk
1/2 teaspoon salt
1 teaspoon sugar
2 tablespoons salad oil
2 tablespoons melted butter
4 teaspoons baking powder

Mix egg yolks, flour, milk, salt, sugar, oil and melted butter. Beat egg whites until stiff, but not dry. Add to first mixture. Just before baking, fold in baking powder.

Bake in pre-heated waffle iron.

Makes 4 waffles, depending on size of waffle iron.

# German Pancake

### Bring to the table in the skillet—attractive!

**4 tablespoons (1/2 stick)
butter
1 cup flour
1 cup milk
4 eggs
Dash of salt**

Heat oven to 425°. Melt butter in a 10-inch cast iron skillet in oven. Add remaining ingredients to melted butter. Stir for 45 seconds. Batter will remain somewhat lumpy.

Bake at 425° for 12 to 15 minutes. Sprinkle with powdered sugar, if you wish. Serve with sausage or bacon. Top with jam, syrup, warm applesauce, or sour cream and fresh fruit or berries.

Serves 4.

## Finnish Oven Pancakes

**This easy breakfast just might become a favorite.**

4 eggs
4 cups milk
2 cups flour
1/4 teaspoon salt
1 teaspoon sugar

Preheat oven to 450°. Mix all ingredients. In each of two 9-by-13-inch pans, melt 1 tablespoon of butter in preheating oven. Remove pans from oven when butter is melted. Divide ingredients into the 2 pans.

Bake at 450° for about 15 minutes, or until crispy brown on edges and golden and bubbly on top. Serve at once with syrup or jam.

Serves 6.

# Egg & Cheese Dishes

# Egg and Cheese Brunch

**Put this together 24 hours before it will be served.**

8 slices bread, crusts
   removed, cubed
1 pound sharp Cheddar
   cheese, grated
1 cup diced ham
6 eggs
1 1/2 cups Half and Half
1/2 teaspoon dry mustard
1/2 teaspoon salt

Butter a 9-by-13-inch pan. Put bread cubes in bottom of pan. Cover with cheese and ham. Combine eggs, Half and Half, mustard and salt. Pour over bread and cheese.

Cover and refrigerate for 24 hours. *Remove from refrigerator 2 hours before baking.*

Bake, uncovered, at 325° for 1 1/2 hours.

Serves 8.

# Company-at-the-Cabin Brunch

18 eggs
1 cup plus 2 tablespoons
   Half and Half
3 tablespoons butter
1 10 1/2-ounce can
   mushroom soup
6-ounce can mushrooms,
   drained
5 ounces (about 1 1/4 cups)
   shredded Cheddar
   cheese
3 to 4 slices bacon, crisply
   fried and crumbled

Combine eggs and Half and Half. Beat. Scramble lightly in butter in large skillet. Put eggs in large, shallow casserole or pan. Pour on soup, mushrooms and cheese. Top with bacon.

Bake at 250° for 45 to 60 minutes. This can be made the night before and refrigerated before baking. If so, bake 1 1/2 hours.

Serves 10 to 12.

## Lazy Day Supper for Two

4 eggs
1/2 cup (or more) Cheddar
   cheese, grated
1/4 cup (scant) whipping
   cream

Butter a small casserole. Sprinkle half of the cheese on bottom of casserole. Put eggs on cheese, as you would for fried eggs. (Line up the eggs so it will be easy to cut after baking.) Sprinkle remaining cheese over eggs. Salt and pepper to taste. Pour cream over all.

Bake, uncovered, at 350° for 15 to 20 minutes, or until center is no longer runny when you shake the casserole.

This recipe can easily be doubled. It can also be quadrupled in a 9-by-13-inch pan, baking for 30 to 40 minutes.

Serves 2.

## Super Simple Supper

**Serve with toast and fresh fruit for a quick meal.**

4 slices bacon, cut up
1 can (1 pound) cream style
   corn, drained
5 eggs, lightly beaten
Seasoned salt

Saute and drain bacon pieces. Add well-drained corn. Simmer until warm.

Add eggs and stir, as for scrambled eggs. Sprinkle to taste with seasoned salt. Serves 4.

# Lake Country Eggs and Sausage

## Prepare the night before.

4 slices white bread, cubed
1 cup shredded sharp cheese
3/4 pound bulk sausage,
    cooked and drained
4 eggs, beaten
1 1/4 cups milk
1/4 teaspoon dry mustard
1/2 10 1/2-ounce can
    mushroom soup
1/4 cup milk

Layer bread, cheese and sausage in a greased 8-by-8-inch pan or casserole. Combine eggs, 1 1/4 cups milk and dry mustard; pour over all.

Cover and refrigerate overnight. Just before popping in the oven, combine soup and 1/4 cup milk. Pour over top of casserole.

Bake, uncovered, at 300° for 1 1/2 hours. A double recipe can be made in a 9-by-13-inch pan.

Serves 4.

## Fluffy Oven Eggs and Bacon

1/2 pound bacon (about 12
    slices)
1/2 cup chopped onion
1/2 cup Bisquick
3 eggs
1 1/4 cups milk
1/4 teaspoon salt
1/8 teaspoon pepper
1/2 cup shredded Cheddar
    or Swiss cheese

Grease 1 1/2-quart round casserole. Cut bacon slices into thirds. Cook and stir bacon in 10-inch skillet over medium heat, until almost crisp. Add onion. Cook, stirring frequently, until bacon is crisp. Drain. Spread bacon and onion in bottom of casserole.

Beat Bisquick, eggs, milk, salt and pepper with hand beater, until almost smooth. Slowly pour egg mixture over bacon; sprinkle with cheese.

Bake in 375° oven, uncovered, until knife inserted in center comes out clean, about 35 minutes.

Serves 4 to 6.

# Impossible Quiche

**Before you take off for the lake, mix butter, milk, Bisquick, eggs and seasonings in a quart jar. Fry the bacon, and crumble into pieces. Chop and saute the onion. Shred the cheese. Place in separate baggies. When you arrive at your cabin, just combine the ingredients and this special supper is ready in 1 hour.**

6 tablespoons butter, melted
12 slices bacon, diced, or
   1 cup cooked ham,
   diced
1/3 cup finely chopped
   onion
1 1/2 cups (6 ounces)
   shredded Swiss or
   Cheddar cheese
1 4-ounce can sliced
   mushrooms (optional)
1 1/2 cups milk
1/2 cup Bisquick
3 eggs
1/4 teaspoon salt
1/8 teaspoon pepper

Lightly grease a 10-inch pie plate. Fry bacon until crisp, and crumble into pan. Saute onion in bacon grease. Sprinkle onion, cheese and mushrooms evenly over bacon. In blender, mix remaining ingredients on high speed for 1 minute, or use hand mixer. Pour into pie plate.

Bake at 350° for 50 to 60 minutes, until golden, and knife comes out clean when inserted in center of quiche. Let stand for 5 minutes before cutting.

Serves 6 to 8.

## Cottage Cheese Spinach Quiche

### No crust needed!

1 cup cottage cheese
10 ounces frozen chopped
   spinach, well-drained
   (squeezed)
3 eggs, beaten
1 scant teaspoon Lawry's
   seasoned salt
Sprinkling of nutmeg
1/2 cup Parmesan cheese
Paprika

Mix all ingredients, except the paprika. Pour into buttered 9-inch pie plate. Sprinkle with paprika.

Bake at 350° for 30 minutes.

Serves 6.

## Shrimp Pie

### Good for Sunday brunch. Serve with a fresh fruit cup and bran muffins.

1 8-ounce can crescent rolls
1 1/2 cups shredded
   Cheddar cheese
3 eggs
1 10 1/2-ounce can cream
   of shrimp soup
1/4 cup chopped celery
1/4 cup chopped green
   pepper
2 tablespoons chopped
   onion
Salt
Pepper

Spread out roll dough in ungreased 9-by-13-inch baking dish. Press over bottom of dish and 1/2 inch up sides to form crust. Sprinkle 1 cup cheese over crust. Beat eggs. Add soup, celery, green pepper, onion, salt and pepper. Pour over cheese and crust. Sprinkle with remaining cheese.

Bake, uncovered, at 375° for 30 to 35 minutes, or until knife inserted off-center comes out clean.
Serves 6 to 8.

## Broccoli Souffle

4 tablespoons butter
1/2 cup chopped onion
2 tablespoons flour
1/2 teaspoon salt
1/2 cup water
8-ounce jar Cheez Whiz
3 eggs, beaten
2 10-ounce packages frozen
    chopped broccoli
Cracker crumbs

Saute butter and onions in pan. Add flour, water and salt. Stir until thick. Add Cheez Whiz. Stir, and let stand.

Mix cooked and drained broccoli with beaten eggs. Pour into cheese mixture. Put into 1 1/2-quart greased casserole. Sprinkle with cracker crumbs.

Bake, uncovered, at 325° for 45 minutes.

Serves 6 to 8.

## Gruyere Oven Omelet

**This recipe can easily be cut in half.**

8 eggs
1 cup milk
1/4 pound Canadian bacon,
    or ham, cut up
2 1/2 cups (10 ounces)
    shredded Gruyere cheese
1/8 teaspoon nutmeg
Sprinkling of salt
Sprinkling of pepper
1 tablespoon melted butter

Beat eggs. Add remaining ingredients, except butter. Pour into buttered 2-quart baking dish. Drizzle top with butter.

Bake, uncovered, at 350° for 40 minutes.

Serves 6 to 8.

## Eggs Albuquerque

**Can be made in advance and stored in the refrigerator.**

1 pint cottage cheese
1/2 cup butter or margarine,
    melted
1/2 cup flour
Dash of salt
1 pound Monterey Jack
    cheese, shredded
10 large eggs
1 teaspoon baking powder
1 8-ounce can chopped
    green chilies

Melt butter. Beat eggs lightly in large bowl. Blend in flour, baking powder and salt. Add melted butter, cleaned chilies, cottage cheese and Monterey Jack cheese.

Bake, uncovered, in 9-by-13-inch baking pan at 400° for 15 minutes and at 350° for 35 to 40 minutes. Cut into squares while warm.

Serves 8 to 10.

## Poached Eggs Supreme

**A good breakfast when people get up at different times.**

1 egg
1 strip bacon
1 piece of toast
1 slice American cheese

Poach egg in water for 4 minutes. Fry bacon. Top buttered toast with cheese, bacon and the poached egg.

Broil for 1 minute, or until cheese starts to melt. Must be eaten immediately.

# Ham 'n' Eggs

## A tasty choice for a birthday brunch.

1 6-ounce box shredded
    hash browns
1 6 1/2-ounce can chopped
    ham
1 cup shredded Cheddar
    cheese
6 eggs, beaten
1 cup milk

Soak hash browns in water until they soften. Drain. Pat into a 9-by-9-inch pan. Layer meat and cheese. Add green pepper or onions, if you desire. Mix eggs and milk. Pour into pan.

Bake at 350° for 45 to 60 minutes.

Serves 4.

# Ham and Egg Pizza

1 tube refrigerated crescent
    rolls
1/4 cup chopped onion
1/4 cup butter
1 cup chopped ham (or
    bacon or turkey)
4 eggs
1/2 cup milk
Salt and pepper
1 cup shredded cheese (Swiss
    or Monterey Jack)

Spread rolls onto pizza pan to make crust. Saute onion in butter. Add ham. Pour over crust.

Combine and beat the eggs, milk, salt and pepper. Pour over ham and onion. Sprinkle cheese on top.

Bake at 350° for 30 minutes, or until brown.

Makes 1 pizza.

# Soups & Sandwiches

## Overnite Barbecue Beef Sandwiches

**This is great for a crowd at the lake. Guests can help themselves when they are hungry. Caution: Make plenty, or the last ones may find an empty pot.**

**4 - 5 pound boneless pork
    or beef roast
1/2 cup water
1 onion, sliced or chopped
1 16-ounce bottle barbecue
    sauce
Buns or French bread**

Cook roast with water in crockpot on low heat for 10 to 12 hours. Remove. Slice thin. Return to crockpot. Add onion and barbecue sauce.

Cook on low for another 4 to 6 hours. Serve on buns or French bread.

## Self-Serve Sandwich

**1 loaf French bread
Lunch meat, sliced
Cheese, sliced
Lettuce
Tomato, sliced
Onion, sliced (optional)**

Cut bread lengthwise. Butter bottom; put mayonnaise on top. Layer cheese, meat, tomato and onion. Top with lettuce. Replace top of bread. Slide back into bread wrapper.

As hunger pangs hit, the loaf can be pulled out, the desired amount sliced off, and the rest returned to the wrapper.

# Hot Ham and Cheese Sandwiches

**The key to this super sandwich is the spread. These sandwiches can be prepared in advance and refrigerated or frozen before baking. Good with potato salad.**

1/2 cup (1 stick) butter or
  margarine
2 tablespoons prepared
  mustard
1 tablespoon poppy seed
1/2 tablespoon Worcester-
  shire sauce
2 tablespoons minced onion
Sliced ham
6 slices Swiss cheese
6 sandwich rolls or rye buns

Combine first 5 ingredients. Open rolls or buns. Spread mixture on top and bottom, as for sandwich. Place ham and cheese in roll. Wrap individually in foil.

Bake at 350° for 15 minutes. Serve immediately. If frozen, thaw before baking.

For appetizers, use Pepperidge Farm Party Rolls. Without separating rolls, slice in half horizontally. Spread with butter mixture. Put ham and cheese on roll slices. Cut into individual servings, either before or after baking.

# Spamwiches

**This mixture can be made ahead and kept in the refrigerator, then used as a spread, hot or cold.**

1 can Spam, cut up
1/4 cup processed cheese,
  cut up
1 small onion, cut up
1 - 2 dill pickles, cut up
3/4 cup mayonnaise

Blend all ingredients in blender or food processor. Spread on hot dog buns. Wrap individual buns in foil. Warm in 350° oven for about 15 minutes.

## Tuna-Cheese Melt

1 6 1/2-ounce can tuna, drained
2 tablespoons finely chopped onion
2 tablespoons diced celery
2 tablespoons mayonnaise or salad dressing
1/4 teaspoon salt
1/4 teaspoon pepper
2 English muffins, split
4 slices tomato
4 slices cheese (Swiss or processed American)

Combine first 6 ingredients. Toast and butter the muffin halves. Layer on each: 1/4 of the tuna mixture, a tomato slice and a slice of cheese.

Bake, uncovered, at 350° for 5 to 7 minutes, or until cheese is melted.

Serves 4.

## Stovetop Hot Beef for Sandwiches

**This keeps well for later re-heating.**

1 chuck roast
Beef bouillon cubes or instant granules
1 package dry onion soup mix
1 cup tomato juice

Brown roast over low heat. Add water to cover. Add bouillon—1 cube or 1 teaspoon for each cup of water used.

Simmer for 3 to 5 hours or until most of liquid is absorbed, and meat can be easily shredded. Shred meat. Add soup mix and juice. Re-heat. Serve on buns.

## Minnetonka Steak Sandwich

**A super-fast meal—try it with fresh sweet corn!**

**3 breakfast steaks (sirloin tip, sliced very thin)**
**French or sourdough bread**

*Dip:*
**1/2 cup butter**
**3 tablespoons Heinz 57 sauce**
**2 tablespoons sliced green onion**

In saucepan, combine butter, sauce and green onion. Cook on low, until butter is melted and onion is soft.

In hot frypan, grill steaks for about 3 minutes (1 1/2 minutes on each side). Dip bread and steak into sauce before making open-faced sandwich.

Serves 3.

## Tuna-Filled Buns

**Make the filling at home, and take it with you.**

**1/4 pound cubed or shredded Cheddar cheese**
**3 hard-cooked eggs, diced**
**1 can tuna**
**2 tablespoons diced green pepper (optional)**
**2 tablespoons diced stuffed olives (optional)**
**2 tablespoons diced sweet pickles (optional)**
**1/2 cup mayonnaise**
**6 buns**

Combine all ingredients. Mix well. Place in 6 buns, and wrap each in foil.

Bake at 250° for 30 minutes. Filling is best when made the day before.

## Relaxed Roast Beef Sandwiches

**Fantastic for several meals at the cabin.**

**4-pound rolled, or rump,
    roast**
**Vegetable oil**
**1 package dry onion soup**
**3 beef bouillon cubes**
**2 cups boiling water**

Brown beef roast in oil on all sides. Dissolve bouillon in water. Add onion soup. Pour over roast.

Roast in covered pan at 250° for about 3 hours, depending upon what doneness you desire. Cool meat. Slice thin. Put back into juice. (Be sure juice covers meat; add water, if necessary.) Let meat marinate at least a day. May be made 3 or 4 days ahead of time and marinated in refrigerator, or may be frozen.

When ready to use, heat slowly on top of stove. Serve as an open-faced sandwich, with sauce on the side.

Serves 10 to 12.

# Hot Dog Toasties

**8 wieners**
**8 slices of bread**
**Soft butter or margarine**
**Mustard, if desired**
**8 slices American cheese**
**1/4 cup butter or margarine,**
    **melted**

Drop wieners into boiling water. Reduce heat. Cover, and simmer for 5 to 8 minutes.

Spread bread with soft butter and mustard. Place bread on cookie sheet or broiler pan. Top each bread slice with a slice of cheese. Place wieners diagonally on cheese. Fold bread over to form a triangle, and secure with toothpicks. Brush with melted butter.

Broil 3 to 4 inches from heat for about 2 minutes, or until golden brown.

Serves 8.

# Spread for Open-Faced Burger

**1 pound hamburger**
**1 teaspoon Worcestershire**
    **sauce**
**1 teaspoon oregano**
**Salt and pepper to taste**
**1 cup shredded Cheddar or**
    **American cheese**

Mix all ingredients. Spread rather thinly on 1/2 hamburger bun or English muffin.

Bake at 300° for 15 to 20 minutes. Watch carefully.

Makes 16 half-bun servings.

## Baked Souper Sandwich

1 1/2 pounds ground beef
1 small onion, chopped
1/2 cup chopped celery
1/2 teaspoon salt
4 cups herb-seasoned
    stuffing cubes
1 1/2 cups milk
2 eggs
1 10 1/2-ounce can cream
    of mushroom soup
1 teaspoon dry mustard
1 cup shredded Cheddar
    cheese

Brown the meat, onion and celery. Drain. Mix in salt. Put stuffing cubes in greased baking pan, 9-by-9-inch or 12-by-8-inch. Top with meat. Beat milk, eggs, soup and mustard. Pour over meat. Sprinkle with cheese.

Bake at 350°, uncovered, for 30 to 40 minutes, or until knife inserted in center comes out clean. Cool for 5 minutes, and cut into squares.

Serves 6.

## Sloppy Joes

**We send this along with our hunters for a filling supper after the shoot.**

1 pound ground beef
1 package French's sloppy
    joe mix
1 6-ounce can tomato paste
1 10 1/2-ounce can chicken
    rice soup
1 can water

Brown hamburger. Drain fat. Add sloppy joe mix, tomato paste, soup and water.

Simmer for 1/2 hour. Serve on buns, toasted if desired.

## Easiest Sloppy Joes

### Or...how come I never heard of this before?

1 - 1 1/2 pounds ground
   beef
Chopped onion (optional)
1 12-ounce bottle chili sauce

Brown ground beef and onion. No seasonings necessary. Drain fat. Add chili sauce, and heat thoroughly.

Fills 4 to 6 buns.


## Sloppy Josephs

1 pound hamburger
1/2 cup chopped onion
1 10 1/2-ounce can chicken
   gumbo soup
3 tablespoons ketchup,
   minimum
1 - 2 tablespoons prepared
   mustard

Brown hamburger and onion. Drain fat. Mix all ingredients.

Simmer for 30 minutes.

Fills 8 hamburger buns.


## Easy Pizzas

1 package English muffins,
   halved
1 jar pizza sauce or
   spaghetti sauce
1 package sliced pepperoni
1 package shredded
   Mozzarella cheese

Place muffin halves on cookie sheet. Spread with pizza sauce. Divide pepperoni among the muffins, covering the pizza sauce. Sprinkle cheese on top.

Bake at 300° for 15 to 20 minutes.

# Open-Faced Hamburgers

**A good way to use up miscellaneous buns, bread, English muffins, etc. It's also a real meat stretcher!**

**1/2 pound ground beef**
**1 small onion, chopped**
**2 - 3 tablespoons milk**
**1/2 teaspoon salt**
**Sprinkle of pepper**
**Bread or buns**

Combine first 5 ingredients. Spread on buttered bread or bun halves, all the way to the edges. (You can also first toast the bread or buns on the bottom side under a broiler.)

Broil until browned. Serve with mustard or ketchup. Easy to make in multiples.

Covers 4 bread or bun pieces.

# Hamburger Goo

**A favorite from a Lake Superior-cabin family.**

**6 slices bacon, chopped**
**1 small onion, chopped**
**1 pound hamburger**
**1 10 1/2-ounce can tomato soup**
**1 cup cubed Velveeta cheese**
**Hamburger buns**

Saute bacon and onion. Add hamburger, and brown. Drain fat. Add soup. Cool. Add cheese. Spread on halves of hamburger buns for open-faced sandwiches.

Bake at 350° for 15 to 20 minutes.

Fills 16 to 20 bun halves.

## Larry's Juicy Hamburgers

**These patties can be mixed, shaped and frozen for later use.**

2 pounds hamburger
1/2 cup grated apple
1/2 teaspoon salt
1/4 teaspoon black pepper
1/4 teaspoon Italian
   seasoning
2 eggs, beaten
1/2 cup cracker crumbs

Combine and blend all
ingredients.

Fry or broil to desired doneness. Serve on buns.

Makes 10 patties.


## Hearty Hamburger Soup

**So good on a "fall-is-near" evening. Keeps for days in the
refrigerator. Freezes well.**

1 1/2 pounds hamburger,
   browned and drained
1 small onion, chopped
4 carrots, chopped
2 stalks celery, chopped
   (use tops, too)
2 10 1/2-ounce cans beef
   consomme
2 soup cans water
1/2 cup barley
1 28-ounce can tomatoes
1 teaspoon salt
1/4 teaspoon pepper
1/4 teaspoon thyme
1 bay leaf

Saute onion lightly in butter.
Brown hamburger. Drain fat.
Combine all ingredients.

Simmer for 1 hour.

Serves at least 8.

# Uncle Ole's Clam-Shrimp Chowder

**This thick Manhattan-style chowder is a favorite of a group of men who hunt and fish together.**

12 slices bacon, cut into
    1/2-inch squares
1 cup chopped onions
1 cup grated carrots
1 cup chopped celery
1 green pepper, finely
    chopped
4 cups milk
6 10 1/2-ounce cans
    potato soup
3 10 1/2-ounce cans tomato
    bisque soup
5 7-ounce cans minced clams
    (do not drain; use juice,
    too)
2 7-ounce cans small whole
    shrimp, drained
1 small jar pimento, cut up

Seasonings:
    Morton's seasoning
    blend, Lawry's seasoned
    salt, parsley, oregano,
    pepper, etc.
1 cup dry vermouth or wine
    (optional)

Fry bacon until crisp. Saute onions, carrots, celery and green pepper until tender. Drain grease.

In a large kettle, combine milk, soups, clams and juice, shrimp and pimento. Simmer, stirring occasionally. Add bacon and vegetables. Season to your own taste. Add vermouth, if desired.

Makes 5 quarts—12 hearty servings.

# Navy Bean Soup

**Good with crackers or cornbread. Freezes well.**

1 pound navy beans
1 teaspoon baking soda
1 ham hock with meat on it
   (or ham leftovers,
   diced)
2 potatoes, peeled and diced
1 medium onion, diced
1 1/2 teaspoons salt

Cover beans with water (1 inch above bean level). Add baking soda. Soak for at least 8 hours.

Drain beans, and add ham hock, potatoes, onion and salt. Barely cover all with water. Cover, and bring to a slow boil. Cook until beans are tender, about 5 hours. Remove bone after ham falls off.

Serves 8.

# Meat Ball Soup

1 pound hamburger
1 tablespoon minced onion
1 egg, beaten
1/2 cup bread crumbs
1/4 teaspoon salt
1/4 teaspoon pepper
1 16-ounce can stewed
   tomatoes
1 8-ounce can tomato sauce
1 8-ounce can mixed
   vegetables
1 tablespoon sugar
1 cup water
1 envelope French onion
   soup mix

Combine hamburger, onion, egg, bread crumbs, salt and pepper. Shape into small balls. Brown in oil. Place remaining ingredients in a large kettle.

Heat to boiling. Add meat balls. Simmer, covered, for 15 minutes.

Serves 6 to 8.

# Gazpacho

**A fine cold soup. Serve with nachos or toast for lunch, or as a first course.**

1 cucumber, peeled, seeded, finely diced
3 tomatoes, peeled, seeded, diced
1 green pepper, diced
1 small can black olives, chopped
1 clove garlic, finely diced (or 1/4 teaspoon garlic powder)
3 stalks celery, diced
2 teaspoons vinegar
1/4 teaspoon salt
1/4 cup salad oil
1 tablespoon snipped parsley
2 teaspoons minced green onions
2 tablespoons lemon juice

Combine cucumber, tomatoes, green pepper, olives, garlic and celery. Combine vinegar, salt, oil, parsley and onions, and mix with vegetables. Pour lemon juice over mixture.

Refrigerate for several hours to blend flavors. Serve in cold bowls or cups. Can garnish with a dollop of sour cream. Keeps for several days in the refrigerator.

Serves 8.

# Salads & Dressings

## Pasta Vegetable Salad

**Very tasty!**

1 7-ounce package macaroni
  rings
2 cups finely chopped
  cabbage
1/2 cup finely diced
  cucumber
1/2 cup finely diced green
  pepper
1 tablespoon finely diced
  onion
1/2 cup sugar
1/4 cup vinegar
1 cup Miracle Whip dressing

Prepare macaroni according to package directions. Drain. Add vegetables. Combine sugar, vinegar and Miracle Whip. Pour over macaroni and vegetables.

Refrigerate in 3-quart container. Keeps well in cooler or refrigerator.

Serves 8.

## Fresh Vegie Salad

**Good for a "potluck" at the lake. Make the day before you'll need it.**

1 head cauliflower
1 bunch broccoli
1 large green pepper,
  chopped
1 sweet red onion, separated
  into rings
1 box cherry tomatoes
1 can sliced water chestnuts
1 can pitted ripe olives
2 envelopes Good Seasons
  Italian salad dressing
  mix

Cut vegetables into bite-sized pieces. Mix salad dressing until creamy, according to package instructions, adding extra tablespoon of oil. Add dressing to vegetables. Toss well. Marinate overnight.

Variations: 1/2 pound sliced fresh mushrooms, and sliced celery. One-half the recipe will serve 4 to 6 for a main course. Good with popovers! Serves 12 to 14.

# Pea Salad

**Good to prepare ahead of time—travels well.**

1 10-ounce package frozen
    peas
1/2 cup diced Cheddar
    cheese
2 hard-cooked eggs, sliced
1/4 cup chopped celery
2 tablespoons chopped onion
3 tomatoes, chopped
1/3 cup mayonnaise
1/2 teaspoon salt
1/4 teaspoon Tabasco sauce
1/8 teaspoon pepper

Mix first 6 ingredients. Combine mayonnaise, salt, pepper and Tabasco. Toss, and chill. Keep refrigerated.

Serves 6.

# Tasty Marinated Vegetable Salad

**Make ahead of time and refrigerate or freeze.**

1 16-ounce can green beans
1 16-ounce can wax beans
1 16-ounce can small whole
    carrots
8 ounces button (whole)
    mushrooms
1 small jar pimento
1 onion, finely chopped

*Marinade:*
1/2 cup vegetable oil
1 1/2 cups sugar
1 cup vinegar
1 teaspoon salt
1 teaspoon celery seed
1/2 teaspoon paprika
Sprinkle of garlic salt

Drain vegetables. Mix together. Mix marinade. Pour over vegetables.

Let stand about 12 hours in refrigerator, stirring occasionally. At this point it may be frozen, or it will keep in refrigerator for several days.

Serves 10.

# Spinach Salad

1 pound fresh spinach,
    washed and drained
Small container of bean
    sprouts
1/4 pound fresh mush-
    rooms, sliced
1 onion, sliced and separated
    into rings
1 8-ounce can water chest-
    nuts, drained and sliced
1/2 pound bacon, fried and
    broken into pieces

Combine spinach, bean sprouts, mushrooms, onion, water chestnuts and bacon.

*Dressing:*
1 cup vegetable oil
1/4 cup vinegar
1/2 cup sugar
1 tablespoon Worcestershire
    sauce
1 medium onion, grated
1/3 cup ketchup
1/2 teaspoon salt

Mix dressing in 1-quart jar. Shake well. Sprinkle over vegetables. Toss.

# Soupy Salad

**Grandpa's favorite luncheon dish. Low in sugar and salt.**

2 carrots, shredded
1 celery stalk, chopped
1 medium tomato, sliced
Cucumber slices
Mayonnaise
Applesauce, natural
Yogurt, plain or vanilla
Cheese, shredded
Coconut

Place carrots, celery, tomato and cucumber in bowl. Mix mayonnaise, applesauce and yogurt. Pour over vegetables. Stir lightly. Garnish with cheese and coconut. Serve with hard-boiled eggs and wheat crackers.

# Overnight Layered Salad

1 head lettuce, finely
    chopped
1/2 cup chopped green
    onion
1 cup chopped celery
    (2 medium stalks)
1 4 1/2-ounce can water
    chestnuts, drained and
    sliced
10 ounces uncooked frozen
    peas, drained
2 medium tomatoes, diced

Place lettuce in a 9-by-13-inch
pan. Layer with remaining
salad ingredients.

*Dressing:*
2 cups mayonnaise
1 teaspoon seasoned salt
1/4 teaspoon garlic powder

Combine dressing ingredients.
Spread over salad.

*Topping:*
1/2 pound cooked bacon,
    diced, or 3/4 to 1 cup
    bacon-flavored protein
    pieces
3 hard-cooked eggs,
    chopped
Parmesan cheese

Top dressing with bacon,
eggs and Parmesan cheese.
Refrigerate overnight.

Serves 10 to 12.

# Summer Salad

### Colorful and crunchy.

10 radishes, chopped
2 cups chopped broccoli
3 cups chopped cauliflower
1/2 cup chopped celery
4 - 6 green onions
    (tops, too)
3 - 4 carrots, sliced into
    coin shape
1/2 cup chopped green
    pepper
Cherry tomatoes
Cucumbers

*Dressing:*
1 cup sour cream
1/2 cup mayonnaise
1/2 package Good Seasons
    Cheese and Garlic
    dressing

Mix dressing and vegetables
20 minutes before serving.

# Fresh Broccoli Salad

1 pound fresh broccoli, cut
    into bite-sized pieces
2 tablespoons chopped
    green onions
2 large tomatoes, chopped

*Dressing:*
1/2 cup mayonnaise
1 tablespoon lemon juice
1/2 teaspoon salt
1/4 teaspoon pepper

Cook broccoli. Chill. Toss
with dressing just before
serving.

# Marinated Carrots

**A tasty cold carrot salad or accompaniment that can be done a day or two before you'll need it.**

2 pounds carrots
1 large onion, thinly sliced
1 large green pepper, cut
    into thin strips
1 can tomato soup
1 cup sugar
1/2 cup salad oil
3/4 cup vinegar
1 teaspoon salt
1/2 teaspoon pepper
1/4 teaspoon dill weed

Peel, slice and cook carrots until just tender. Drain, and cool. Put carrots, onion and green pepper in 2-quart bowl or jar. Mix together in a saucepan, the soup and all ingredients following it. Bring to a boil. Stir. Pour hot soup mixture over vegetables. Cover.

Refrigerate. Make at least 12 hours before serving. It keeps well for several days.

Serves 10.

# Carrot-Tuna-Shoestring Salad

**An unusual combination of ingredients that is excellent.**

6 carrots, grated
1 can tuna, drained
1/2 cup diced celery
1 small onion, chopped
1 cup mayonnaise
2 tablespoons French
    dressing
2 tablespoons sugar
1 cup (or more) shoestring
    potatoes

Mix carrots, tuna, celery and onion. Mix mayonnaise, French dressing and sugar. Toss with vegetables.

Chill for a few hours before serving. Just before serving, stir in shoestring potatoes.

Serves 6.

## Three-Bean Salad

**Almost everyone makes this and likes it. We include it in case you forgot how to make the dressing!**

1 can green beans, drained
1 can wax beans, drained
1 can kidney beans, drained
1 small green pepper,
   chopped
1 cup sliced celery
1/2 cup chopped onion
1 jar button mushrooms
1/2 cup vegetable oil
3/4 cup sugar
2/3 cup vinegar
1/2 teaspoon salt
1/2 teaspoon pepper

Combine vegetables. Combine oil, sugar, vinegar, salt and pepper. Pour over vegetables.

Marinate overnight before serving. Travels well and keeps for days. For lunch, serve on a bed of shredded lettuce, with toast.

Serves 10 to 12.

## Calypso Salad

1 12-ounce can mexicorn,
   drained
4 cups shredded cabbage
1/4 cup finely chopped
   onion
1/4 cup cubed sharp
   Cheddar cheese
1/4 cup sliced black olives

*Dressing:*
1 cup mayonnaise
2 tablespoons white vinegar
2 tablespoons sugar
1 tablespoon prepared
   mustard
1/4 teaspoon celery seed
Salt to taste

Combine dressing ingredients. Mix well with other ingredients. Let stand 1/2 hour before serving.

Serves 8 to 10.

## Mexican Chip Salad

### It's crunchy, tasty and filling!

2 pounds ground beef
1 envelope taco seasoning
1 large bag taco chips
3 tomatoes, chopped
1 pound Cheddar cheese or
    processed cheese, grated
1 large head lettuce,
    chopped

Brown ground beef and drain. Add taco seasoning. Mix well.

Just before serving, mix all ingredients in large bowl. Black olives and chopped onion may be added for additional color and flavor. This salad does not keep well.

Serves 6.

## Taco Salad

1 pound hamburger
8 ounces grated Cheddar
    cheese
1 can kidney beans, drained
1 or 2 tomatoes, chopped
Chopped onion to taste
1 head lettuce, torn up
1 bag (1/2 pound) Doritos,
    crushed
2 chopped avocadoes
    (optional)
Thousand Island Dressing,
    about 1 cup
Taco sauce to taste

Brown hamburger. Drain fat. Chill. First 5 ingredients can be combined a few hours before serving. At last minute, add lettuce, Doritos and avocadoes. Mix taco sauce into Thousand Island dressing to taste. Toss with all ingredients.

Serves 10.

## Favorite Sauerkraut Salad

1 can sauerkraut, rinsed
    and drained
1 can green beans, drained
1 can wax beans, drained
2 cups sliced celery
1 medium onion, chopped
1 small jar pimento
1 green pepper, chopped
1 tablespoon vegetable oil
1 cup vinegar
1 1/2 cups sugar

Combine vegetables. Combine oil, vinegar and sugar. Bring to a boil. Cool. Pour over vegetables.

Refrigerate. Can make a day or two in advance.

Serves 10 to 12.

## Scandinavian Salad

**This may also be served on hearty dark bread, on a lettuce leaf, as an open-faced sandwich.**

1 box frozen peas
3 carrots, grated
6 ounces small shrimp,
    frozen or canned
1/2 cup mayonnaise or
    salad dressing
Salt
Pepper
Dill weed
Squeeze of lemon juice

Combine peas, carrots and shrimp. To mayonnaise, add salt, pepper, dill weed, and lemon juice to taste. Combine with peas, carrots and shrimp.

Serves 4.

## Middle Eastern Lentil Salad

**A wonderful vegetarian protein source with a Mideast flavor.**

1 cup dried lentils
4 cups water
1/2 cup olive oil
5 tablespoons fresh lemon
    juice
3 tablespoons minced fresh
    parsley
2 cloves garlic, crushed
3/4 teaspoon ground cumin
1 teaspoon salt
1/4 teaspoon freshly ground
    pepper

Bring lentils and water to a boil. Reduce heat. Simmer, uncovered, until lentils are firm-tender (about 30 minutes).

Whisk remaining ingredients in a bowl. Drain lentils well. While still warm, add lentils to the dressing. Toss well. Arrange on a plate. May sprinkle with coriander (optional).

Refrigerate, covered, for at least 3 hours or overnight.

## Tuna Salad

2 6 1/2-ounce cans tuna,
    drained
3 green onions, chopped
3 stalks celery, chopped

*Dressing:*
1/2 cup mayonnaise
1/2 cup sour cream
2 tablespoons vinegar
2 tablespoons sugar
1 teaspoon salt
1 cup chow mein noodles

Combine dressing ingredients. Toss with tuna, onions and celery. When ready to serve, add chow mein noodles. Serve on lettuce.

Serves 4.

## Make-Ahead Seafood Salad

**This main course salad makes a delightful lunch or supper,
with chips and relishes.**

3/4 pound white bread slices
1 7-ounce can crab meat,
   flaked
1 7-ounce can shrimp
2 hard-cooked eggs
1 1/2 cups mayonnaise
1/2 teaspoon salt
4 teaspoons lemon juice
1/4 teaspoon dill weed
Sprinkle of curry

Trim bread crusts from
bread. Cut bread into
1/2-inch cubes. Mix with
crab, shrimp and eggs. Add
seasonings to mayonnaise.
Mix well. Combine all ingredients. Pat into 9-by-9-inch
pan.

Chill overnight. Cut into
squares. Serve on lettuce.
Garnish for color with
paprika or snipped parsley.

Serves 6 to 8.

## Freelancer's Rice Salad

**Leftover rice can be used as a base for a salad of leftovers.
Your own taste, and available ingredients, will determine
the outcome.**

2 cups cooked rice
1/4 cup salad dressing
   (French, Italian, etc.)
Seasoned salt, to taste
Vegetables of your choice
   (tomatoes, green pep-
   pers, cauliflower, zucchini, celery, broccoli,
   etc.)

Mix rice, dressing and seasonings. Add chopped and diced
vegetables.

# Shrimp Salad

**This can be made the day before serving.**

2 cups shell macaroni,
  cooked
1 green pepper, chopped
1 medium onion, diced
2 10-ounce packages frozen
  small shrimp
1 small jar stuffed olives,
  sliced

*Dressing:*
3 egg yolks, well-beaten
1 1/4 cups sugar
3/4 cup vinegar
1 tablespoon flour
1 tablespoon cornstarch
Salt and pepper to taste

Cook dressing ingredients until thick. Cool. Mix with salad ingredients. Cover.

Refrigerate.

Serves 8 to 10.

# Coca-Cola Salad

**Refreshing...different.**

1 3-ounce package orange
  Jell-o
1 3-ounce package cream
  cheese, softened
10 ounces Coca-Cola
1/2 cup chopped nuts

Blend dry Jell-o into cream cheese. Heat Coca-Cola to boiling point. Pour over mixture. Mix. Add nuts. Pour into mold or bowl. Let sit for 1 to 2 hours before putting in refrigerator. Salad should separate into three layers.

Serves 4.

## Cherry Delight

1  6-ounce package cherry
    Jell-o
1  8-ounce container Cool
    Whip
1  can pitted sweet cherries
    (reserve juice for liquid
    in Jell-o)

Prepare Jell-o according to
package directions. When
partially set, whip Jell-o and
Cool Whip together until
smooth. Stir in drained
cherries. Chill.

Serves 8 to 10.

## Easy Fruit Salad

1  13 1/2-ounce can chunk
    pineapple, drained
1  16-ounce can pears or
    peaches, drained and
    cubed
1  11-ounce can mandarin
    oranges, drained
1  22-ounce can peach or
    apricot pie filling

Mix all ingredients. Refrigerate several hours before
serving.

This recipe is very flexible. It
can be used successfully with
miniature marshmallows,
sliced bananas, grapes, melon
pieces, and many other fresh
fruits...experiment!

Serves 6 to 8.

## Mandarin-Orange Salad

2 11-ounce cans mandarin
    oranges
2 cups liquid
1 6-ounce package orange
    gelatin
1 pint orange sherbet

Drain juice from oranges. Add water to juice to make 2 cups liquid. Bring liquid to a boil. Pour over gelatin. Stir until dissolved. Add sherbet.

Allow mixture to partially set. Stir in oranges. Pour into 9-by-9-inch glass pan. Chill until firm. Cut into squares. Serve on lettuce.

Serves 9.

## Mandarin-Cashew Salad

### Delicious!

2 heads lettuce, broken into
    bite-sized pieces
3 11-ounce cans mandarin
    oranges, drained
1 cup salted cashew nuts
1 medium onion, thinly
    sliced and divided into
    rings
Oil and vinegar salad dressing

Combine lettuce, oranges, nuts and onion rings. Toss with oil and vinegar dressing, just before serving.

Serves 10 to 12.

## Blueberry Salad

**Easy, rather sweet, purple, and very good.**

2 3-ounce packages straw-
    berry Jell-o
1 can blueberry pie filling
1 cup sour cream, at room
    temperature

Dissolve Jell-o in 2 cups boiling water. Cool. Add blueberry filling and sour cream.
Mix thoroughly. Chill.

Serves 8 to 10.

## Fruity Strawberry Salad

**A refreshing salad, dense with fruit, that does not easily melt
on a plate with warm foods.**

6 ounces strawberry-flavored
    gelatin
2 cups boiling water
10-ounce package frozen
    strawberries, partially
    thawed
1 20-ounce can crushed
    pineapple, drained
2 cups mashed bananas
    (3 large bananas)

Dissolve gelatin in boiling
water. Add strawberries. Stir
until strawberries thaw. Add
drained pineapple and
bananas. Chill.

Serves 10 to 12.

## Quick Molded Salad

1 3-ounce package lemon
  Jell-o
1 10-ounce package frozen
  raspberries
1 10-ounce can mandarin
  oranges, drained

Dissolve Jell-o in 1 cup boiling water. Add raspberries. Add mandarin oranges. Mix well. Pour into 1-quart mold. Chill. Salad is ready to serve in about 2 hours.

Serves 6 to 8.

## Simple Low-Calorie Salad

1 box (2 envelopes) D-Zerta
  lime gelatin dessert
1 20-ounce can crushed
  pineapple, unsweetened
1 20-ounce can pineapple
  chunks, unsweetened
1 1/2 cups boiling water
1/2 cup cold water
1/2 - 1 cup nuts

Dissolve gelatin (both envelopes) in boiling water. Add cold water. Stir in crushed and chunky pineapple. Add nuts. Pour into 9-by-9-inch glass pan.

Chill until firm. Cut into squares. Serve on lettuce. Garnish with non-dairy whipped topping, if desired.

Serves 9.

## Frozen Fruit Salad

**1-pound carton sour cream**
**1/2 cup sugar**
**2 tablespoons lemon juice**
**1 8-ounce jar maraschino**
    **cherries, drained and**
    **halved**
**1 16-ounce can chunky fruit**
    **cocktail, light**
**1 20-ounce can crushed**
    **pineapple, unsweetened**
**1 cup chopped nuts**
**3 - 4 bananas**

Mix all ingredients. Place paper baking cups in muffin tins. Fill 3/4 full.

Freeze until solid. Remove and store in freezer bag. Use as needed.

Makes 36 servings.


## French Dressing

### A favorite!

**1 cup salad oil**
**1 cup sugar**
**1/2 cup vinegar**
**1 small onion, diced**
**1 1/2 teaspoons salt**
**1/2 cup ketchup**
**1/2 cup chili sauce**

Combine all ingredients. Mix well.

Store in jar in refrigerator.

## Strawberry-Sour Cream Dressing

**Delicious mixed with fruit as a salad, or as a topping
on fresh fruit dessert.**

2 cups sour cream
1 teaspoon salt
1/2 cup frozen strawberries,
   thawed

Combine sour cream and salt.
Fold strawberries into sour
cream mixture.


## Cole Slaw with Cooked Dressing

**This should be made several hours before eating, so it is ideal
to make in the morning for the evening meal.**

1 small head cabbage,
   shredded
1 small onion, diced
2 carrots, shredded
1 tablespoon celery seed
Salt to taste

*Dressing:*
3/4 cup vinegar
1 1/4 cups sugar
3/4 cup vegetable oil

Combine cabbage, onion,
carrots, celery seed and salt.

Combine dressing ingredients
in saucepan. Bring to a boil.
Pour over cabbage mixture.

Refrigerate at least 3 hours.

## Frozen Cole Slaw

**This will also keep well in the refrigerator for a week,
if you choose not to freeze it.**

1 medium head cabbage,
   shredded
1 teaspoon salt
2 stalks celery, chopped
1 green pepper, chopped
2 carrots, grated

*Dressing:*
1 cup vinegar
1/2 cup water
1 1/2 cups sugar
1 teaspoon celery seed
1 teaspoon mustard seed

Mix salt with shredded cabbage. Let stand 1 hour. Drain any liquid. Add celery, pepper and carrots.

Combine vinegar, water, sugar, celery seed and mustard seed. Boil for 1 minute. Cool and pour over cabbage. Freeze. Remove from freezer about 2 hours before serving.

Serves 6 to 8.

## Overnite Cole Slaw

**A cole slaw with good staying power.**

1 head cabbage, grated
2 carrots, grated
1 small green pepper, diced
1 small jar pimento, cut up
1 small onion, finely grated

*Dressing:*
1 cup sugar
1 cup vinegar
1/2 teaspoon salt
1/2 teaspoon celery seed

Mix first 5 ingredients.

Combine dressing ingredients. Bring to a boil. While hot, pour over vegetables. Let stand overnight.

# Cabbage Slaw

1 head cabbage, shredded
1 green pepper, chopped
1 2-ounce jar pimento,
    cut up

*Dressing:*
1 1/4 cups sugar
3/4 cup vinegar
1 teaspoon celery seed
1 teaspoon mustard seed
1/2 teaspoon salt

Mix salad ingredients. Combine dressing ingredients. Toss with salad.

Refrigerate overnight.

Serves 10 to 12.

# Cabin German Potato Salad

1 chopped onion
5 - 6 bacon strips, cut into
    pieces
2 16-ounce cans German
    potato salad
2 tablespoons brown sugar

Brown onion and bacon pieces. Add potato salad.

Heat thoroughly. Sprinkle brown sugar on top. Heat 5 minutes longer.

Serves 5 to 6.

# Old-Fashioned Potato Salad

**Very good—and this recipe eliminates the guessing when
seasoning. Make it early in the day, and have this part of the
dinner finished!**

**2 1/2 - 3 cups cooked
    potatoes, peeled and
    cubed
1 teaspoon sugar
1 teaspoon vinegar
1/2 cup sliced celery
2 hard-cooked eggs,
    chopped
1/3 cup finely chopped
    onion
1 teaspoon salt
3/4 teaspoon celery seed
3/4 cup mayonnaise
Parsley and 1 hard-cooked
    egg for garnish**

Sprinkle potatoes, while
warm, with vinegar and
sugar. Toss with a fork. Set
aside for 1 hour or so.

Add celery and eggs to
potatoes. Mix onion and
seasonings into mayonnaise.
Toss to mix. Refrigerate to
thoroughly chill.

Serves 6.

# Main Dishes

## Calico Bean Casserole

**This is a favorite meal of many cabin chefs.**

1/2 pound bacon, diced
2 pounds ground beef
1 cup chopped onions
1 cup chopped celery
1 16-ounce can baked beans
    in tomato sauce
1 15 1/2-ounce can kidney
    beans
1 16-ounce can lima beans,
    drained
1 15 1/2-ounce can butter
    beans, drained
1 cup ketchup
3 tablespoons vinegar
1 teaspoon dry mustard
1/2 cup brown sugar
1 teaspoon salt

Fry bacon pieces and remove from grease. Brown beef. Add onions and celery at end of browning. In a baking dish combine remaining ingredients, including bacon. Add beef mixture.

Bake, covered, at 350° for 45 minutes. You may also cook in a crock pot on low heat for 6 to 8 hours. Keeps refrigerated for days, and freezes well.

Serves 10 to 12.

## Corn Sausage Casserole

1 pound bulk pork
    sausage
4 eggs, beaten
2 1/2 cups cream style corn
1 cup bread crumbs
1 teaspoon salt
1/8 teaspoon pepper
1/4 - 1/2 cup ketchup

Brown sausage. Drain. Mix all ingredients, except ketchup. Pour into greased 10-by-6-inch casserole.

Bake, uncovered, at 350° for 30 minutes. Spread ketchup on top. Bake for 10 minutes more.

Serves 6.

# Dried Beef Casserole

## Allow at least 4 hours for this recipe.

1 10 1/2-ounce can cream
   of mushroom soup
1 cup milk
1 cup grated Cheddar cheese
3 tablespoons finely
   chopped onion
1 cup elbow macaroni,
   cooked
1/4 pound dried beef,
   soaked in boiling water
   and drained
2 hard-cooked eggs, diced

Stir soup to creamy consistency. Stir in remaining ingredients, except eggs. Gently fold in eggs. Put in buttered 2-quart casserole. Refrigerate at least 3 hours, or overnight.

Bake, uncovered, for 1 hour at 350°.

Serves 4 to 6.

# Easy Chili

1 pound hamburger,
   seasoned
1 onion, chopped
1 cup chopped celery
2 cans kidney beans or
   chili beans, drained
1 48-ounce can tomato juice
1 teaspoon chili powder
   (optional)

Brown onion with hamburger. Drain grease. Combine all ingredients in large kettle. Simmer for at least 1 hour.

Serves 4 to 6.

# Chicken-Vegetable-French-Fry Casserole

**This provides meat, potatoes and vegetables in one dish. Put together ahead of time, and it's ready to eat 35 minutes after popping in the oven.**

**2 fryer chickens, cut up**
**1/4 cup (1/2 stick) butter**
**1/4 cup flour**
**1 teaspoon salt**
**2 cups reserved chicken broth**
**1 10 1/2-ounce can cream of celery soup**
**1 10-ounce package frozen peas and carrots**
**1/2 cup (1 stick) butter**
**1 pound box frozen French fries**
**Parmesan cheese**

Cook, cool and de-bone chicken. Save 2 cups of broth. (This much could be done before going to the cabin.) In a buttered 9-by-13-inch pan, or lasagna pan, put good-sized pieces of chicken.

Melt butter; add flour, salt, broth and soup. Cook until thick and smooth. Cook peas and carrots for 3 minutes. Drain. Mix with sauce and pour over chicken.

Melt stick of butter, and stir frozen French fries in it until coated. Place on top of other ingredients. Sprinkle generously with Parmesan.

Bake, uncovered, at 450° for 20 to 25 minutes. If it has been put together earlier and refrigerated, bake for 35 minutes.

Serves 8.

## Hamburger-Wild Rice Casserole

**This can be refrigerated or frozen before it is baked.**

1 cup wild rice, washed
1/4 cup chopped onion
1 1/2 pounds ground beef
1 10 1/2-ounce can cream
    of mushroom soup
1 10 1/2-ounce can cream
    of chicken soup
1 can mushrooms, drained
1 can water chestnuts,
    drained and sliced
2 beef bouillon cubes in
    1 cup boiling water

Put rice in kettle, and cover with 4 cups boiling water. Simmer for 5 minutes. Remove from heat, and let stand 15 minutes before draining. Brown onion and ground beef. Drain grease. Combine all ingredients. Season to taste with salt, onion salt, paprika, celery salt, etc.

Bake at 350° for 1 1/2 hours, covering for first half of baking, then uncovering. This 'holds well' in oven—it can bake for up to 3 hours.

Serves 12.

## Easy Stove-Top Stew For 4

1 pound stew meat
1 teaspoon salt
1 10 1/2-ounce can tomato
    soup
1 can water
3 carrots
3 potatoes
3 small onions

Brown meat in small amount of cooking oil in a large frying pan. Add salt. Stir in soup and water.

Cover, and simmer 1 1/2 hours. Add chopped carrots, potatoes and onions. Cook for 30 minutes more. If there is not enough juice, add water. Serves 4.

## Can Opener Casserole

1 10 1/2-ounce can cream
    of mushroom soup
1 10 1/2-ounce can cream
    of chicken soup
1 small can evaporated milk
2 6 1/2-ounce cans boned
    chicken
1 4 1/2-ounce can mush-
    rooms, drained
1 cup chopped celery
    (sauteed in butter)
2 cups Chinese noodles
Slivered almonds
1 small jar pimento

Combine first 7 ingredients, and place in 1 1/2-quart casserole.

Bake, covered, at 350° for 1 hour. Before serving, garnish with slivered almonds and red pimento.

Serves 6 to 8.

## Cabin Stew

### No need to brown the meat.

2 pounds stew meat, cubed
1 20-ounce can tomatoes
1 box frozen peas
6 carrots, sliced
3 small onions, chopped,
    or 1 small jar onions
    and juice
1 cup celery, sliced
3 medium potatoes, diced
2 tablespoons sugar
1 tablespoon salt
1/4 teaspoon pepper
1/4 cup quick tapioca
1 5-ounce can water chest-
    nuts, drained and sliced
1/4 cup dry red wine

Put all ingredients in casserole. Stir to blend. Cover.

Bake at 275° for 5 hours or longer. Freezes well.

Serves 8.

# Hunters' Stew

## A traditional fall meal at the lake.

4 slices bacon, cut into
1-inch pieces
1 tablespoon butter or
margarine
1 pound lean beef for
stewing, cut into 1-inch
cubes
2 large onions (2 cups),
chopped
3 medium-sized apples
(2 cups), pared,
quartered, cored
and chopped
1 10 1/2-ounce can beef
broth
2 cups water
1 1/2 teaspoons salt
2 cups carrots, pared and
diced
1 pound Polish sausage, cut
into 1 1/2-inch lengths
1 small head cabbage
(4 cups), shredded

Cook bacon in a heavy kettle or Dutch oven until crisp. Remove with a slotted spoon, and set aside. Drain on paper toweling. Add butter to drippings in kettle. Add beef, part at a time, turning to brown well on all sides. Stir in onion and apple. Cook about 5 minutes or until apple is tender. Add beef broth, water and salt. Cover.

Simmer 1 hour and 20 minutes. Add carrots and sausages. Simmer 30 minutes longer. Add cabbage and reserved bacon. Simmer 10 minutes, or until cabbage is tender.

May be cooked in a crock pot for 6 hours on high, or 8 hours on low. All ingredients may be placed in the crock pot at the same time. Variation: Omit the cabbage, and use 1 1/2 pounds beef and 1/2 pound Polish sausage.

## Old Tyme Beef Stew

**This freezes well. You might want to double the recipe.**

2 pounds beef chuck, cut
    into bite-sized pieces
2 tablespoons shortening
4 cups boiling water
1 tablespoon lemon juice
1 teaspoon Worcestershire
    sauce
1 clove garlic, on toothpick
1 medium onion, sliced
1 - 2 bay leaves
1 tablespoon salt
1 teaspoon sugar
1/2 teaspoon pepper
4 large carrots, sliced
4 large potatoes, diced

Brown meat in hot shortening. Add all ingredients except carrots and potatoes. Cover. Simmer for 2 hours, stirring occasionally. Remove bay leaves and garlic. Add carrots and potatoes.

Cover and cook 30 minutes, or until vegetables are done. Remove meat and vegetables. Skim excess fat. Thicken liquid for gravy by mixing 1/2 cup water and 1/4 cup flour, and adding slowly to meat stock. Cook for 5 minutes, until thickened, and pour over vegetables—or vegetables can be returned to gravy and mixed together.

Make at home, and take to the cabin for re-heating.

# Chow Mein

## May be made ahead and re-heated.

2 pounds chow mein meat
    (pork and veal)
1 1/2 cups (or more)
    chopped celery
1 large onion, chopped
1 can bean sprouts, drained
    (save the juice)
1 can sliced water chestnuts
Fresh mushrooms, sliced
1 beef bouillon cube, in
    1/2 cup boiling water
1 10 1/2-ounce can cream
    of mushroom soup
1 can mushroom steak sauce
1 tablespoon molasses
3 tablespoons soy sauce
2 tablespoons cornstarch

Brown meat, seasoning with quite a bit of pepper, but no salt. Add remaining ingredients, except cornstarch.

Simmer, covered, 1 to 1 1/4 hours. Thicken with cornstarch and small portion of bean sprout juice. Serve over rice or chow mein noodles.

Serves 6 to 8.

# Chow Mein Hot Dish

1 pound ground beef
2 cups diced celery
3 medium-sized onions,
    chopped
1 cup raw rice
2 1/2 cups hot water
1 10 1/2-ounce can cream
    of mushroom soup
4 tablespoons soy sauce
1 tablespoon brown sugar
1/2 pound salted peanuts

Saute beef, celery and onions. Drain grease. Add remaining ingredients, except peanuts.

Bake, uncovered, at 400° for 1 hour. After 45 minutes of baking, cover top with salted peanuts. Continue baking for another 15 minutes.

Serves 8 to 10.

## Chopstix Tuna

1 10 1/2-ounce can cream
    of mushroom soup
1/4 cup water
2 cups chow mein noodles
1 6 1/2-ounce can white
    tuna, water packed,
    drained
1 cup sliced celery
1/2 cup salted cashews
1/4 cup chopped onion
Dash of pepper

Combine soup and water.
Add 1 cup noodles, tuna,
celery, onion, cashews and
pepper. Place in 1 1/2-quart
casserole. Sprinkle 1 cup
noodles over the top.

Bake, uncovered, at 375° for
15 minutes. May garnish with
mandarin orange slices.

Serves 4.

## Ground Beef Stir-Fry

**Excellent for "drop-ins" or when you don't know what time
your eaters will arrive.**

2 tablespoons oil
1 1/2 pounds ground beef
1/4 cup soy sauce
1 green pepper, cut up
3 carrots, thinly sliced
2 onions, sliced and cut
    into 1/2 rings
4 stalks celery, sliced
    diagonally
Fresh or canned mushrooms
1 tablespoon cornstarch
1/2 cup beef consomme
    (freeze the rest for
    later use)

Stir-fry ground beef in hot oil
in frypan or wok (450° in
electric frypan). When meat
is brown, add soy sauce and
vegetables. Cover, and cook
5 to 8 minutes, until tender-
crisp, stirring occasionally.

Dissolve cornstarch in consomme. Add to meat and
vegetables to thicken. Season
with salt and pepper. Serve
over cooked rice.

Serves 6.

# Cheeseburger Pie

1 pound ground beef
1 1/2 cups chopped onion
1/2 teaspoon salt
1/4 teaspoon pepper
1 cup (4 ounces) shredded
    Cheddar cheese
1 1/2 cups milk
3/4 cup Bisquick
3 eggs

Lightly grease a 10-inch pie plate. Cook and stir ground beef and onion until beef is brown. Drain. Stir in salt and pepper. Spread in pie plate. Sprinkle with cheese.

Beat remaining ingredients until smooth, 15 seconds in blender on high speed or 1 minute with hand beater. Pour into pie plate.

Bake at 400° about 30 minutes, until golden brown. Let stand 5 minutes before cutting. Refrigerate any remaining pie.

Note: If using a 9-inch pie plate, decrease milk to 1 cup, Bisquick to 1/2 cup and eggs to 2.

Serves 6 to 8.

# Good and Easy Spaghetti Sauce

1 package spaghetti sauce
    mix
1 pound hamburger,
    browned
Black olives, sliced
Celery, sliced
Fresh mushrooms, sliced
Green pepper, chopped

Follow directions on the package of spaghetti sauce mix. Add the rest of the ingredients to it. Serve over cooked spaghetti.

# Spaghetti Pie

### A do-ahead main dish.

6 ounces spaghetti
2 tablespoons butter
1/2 cup grated Parmesan
    cheese
2 eggs, well-beaten
1 pound hamburger
1/2 cup finely chopped
    green onion
1/4 cup chopped green
    pepper
1/2 cup cut-up tomatoes
    (fresh or canned)
1 6-ounce can tomato paste
1 teaspoon sugar
1 teaspoon oregano
1/2 teaspoon garlic salt
1 cup cottage cheese
1/2 cup shredded Mozza-
    rella cheese

Stir butter into spaghetti, which has been cooked, drained and rinsed. Add Parmesan and eggs. Form this into a crust in a buttered 10-inch pie pan.

Cook beef, onion and green pepper. Drain. Stir in tomatoes, tomato paste, sugar, oregano and garlic salt. Spread cottage cheese over spaghetti crust. Cover with meat and tomato mixture. Top with Mozzarella cheese. At this point, pie can be frozen or refrigerated.

Bake, uncovered, at 350° for 30 minutes (longer, if frozen), or until bubbly. Recipe can easily be doubled.

Serves 6.

## Make-Ahead Spaghetti Sauce/Chili Base

### Freeze in meal-sized containers.

4 pounds ground beef
2 cups chopped onions
1 cup chopped green pepper
2 cups chopped celery
16 ounces tomato sauce
12 ounces tomato paste
4 cups tomatoes (fresh or
     canned)
2 tablespoons sugar
2 teaspoons salt
2 cloves garlic (on tooth-
     picks for removal)
2 bay leaves
1/2 teaspoon oregano

Brown the beef. Midway through the browning, add onions, pepper and celery. When meat is browned, drain the grease. Add remaining ingredients. Simmer for 2 hours. Remove garlic and bay leaves.

Freeze this spaghetti sauce, if you wish. To transform this into chili, add chili powder and cans of chili beans or kidney beans (drained) to taste.

## Meat Balls

1 bouillon cube
1/2 cup hot water
1/2 cup milk
1 cup soft bread crumbs
2 pounds ground beef
1/2 cup chopped onion, or
     2 tablespoons instant
     onion
1 teaspoon sugar
1 teaspoon seasoned salt
1 egg
1 10 1/2-ounce can cream
     of mushroom soup

Combine bouillon cube and hot water. Add other ingredients, except soup. Make small meatballs. Place on cookie sheet.

Bake in 350° oven for 30 minutes. Place meatballs in baking dish, and spread with slightly diluted soup. Bake 30 minutes more. Freezes well.

Serves 6 to 8.

# One-Pan Spaghetti

**Time-saver spaghetti! One pan and no precooking of noodles. Celery loaf or Italian bread goes well with this dish.**

1 pound ground beef
1/2 cup chopped onion, or
   2 tablespoons onion
   flakes
1 9-ounce can whole
   tomatoes
1 18-ounce can tomato juice
1 8-ounce can tomato sauce
1 1/2 teaspoons sugar
1 1/2 teaspoons oregano
3/4 teaspoon garlic powder
1 teaspoon Worcestershire
   sauce
1/2 teaspoon salt
1/2 7-ounce package
   spaghetti, uncooked
   and broken

Brown beef and onion in a large saucepan. Drain fat. Add the tomatoes, tomato juice, tomato sauce, and the seasonings. Bring the mixture to a boil. Add the uncooked spaghetti, and lower heat to simmer.

Cover tightly, and simmer for 40 minutes, stirring occasionally. Uncover, and simmer for 15 minutes. Or bake, covered, at 325° for 1 hour, stirring occasionally. Uncover, and bake 1/2 hour longer. Parmesan cheese can be sprinkled on top just before serving.

Serves 4 to 6.

# Meat and Macaroni Dinner

1 pound ground beef
1/4 cup chopped onion
1 cup elbow macaroni,
   cooked and drained
1 10 1/2-ounce can
   Cheddar cheese soup
1/3 cup water
1/4 teaspoon pepper

Cook meat and onion in large skillet until onion is tender. Drain fat. Add remaining ingredients. Heat thoroughly, and serve.

Serves 4.

# Do-Ahead Lasagna

**This recipe can be made ahead of time and left in the refrigerator all day. The uncooked noodles make it super for saving—time and pans!**

1 pound ground beef
1 tablespoon instant chopped
   onion
2 teaspoons salt
1 tablespoon sugar
1 teaspoon chili powder
1 teaspoon garlic salt
1 1/2 teaspoons basil or
   oregano
1 12-ounce can tomato paste
1 15-ounce can tomato sauce
3 1/2 cups water
3/4 pound (2 1/4 cups)
   shredded cheese, (American or Mozzarella)
3/4 pound lasagna noodles,
   uncooked

Brown ground beef with onion and seasonings. Add tomato paste, tomato sauce and water. Bring to a boil, simmer 10 minutes. (Mixture will be thin.)

In 9-by-13-inch baking pan, ladle about 1 1/2 cups sauce. Cover sauce with 4 uncooked noodles. Ladle more sauce to cover noodles. Sprinkle 1/3 of cheese over sauce. Make 3 layers like this. Cover with foil.

Bake at 350° for 1 1/2 hours, or for 2 hours if it has been refrigerated.

# Park Rapids Goo

**Fast and easy.**

1 pound ground beef
1 small onion, chopped
   (optional)
1 14 3/4-ounce can Franco-
   American spaghetti
Parmesan cheese

Fry hamburger with onion. Drain grease. Add spaghetti. Heat thoroughly. Sprinkle with Parmesan cheese.

Serves 4.

# Pot Roast Meat Loaf

1 pound lean ground beef
2/3 cup evaporated milk
1/3 cup fine bread crumbs
1/4 cup ketchup
1 teaspoon salt
2 teaspoons Worcestershire
  sauce
Dash of pepper
2 teaspoons dried parsley
  flakes
3 medium potatoes, peeled
  and sliced
3 medium onions, sliced
3 medium carrots, sliced
1 teaspoon salt

Combine all ingredients, except parsley flakes, vegetables and salt. Shape into loaf. Place in 9-by-13-inch pan. Place vegetables in layers around meat. Sprinkle with parsley flakes and salt. Cover with foil.

Bake at 375° for 1 hour, or until vegetables are tender. Remove foil. Bake 10 minutes longer.

Serves 4.

# Good Neighbor's Hot Dish with Sour Cream

1 cup chopped onion
2 tablespoons margarine
1 1/2 pounds ground beef
3 cups medium noodles,
  uncooked
3 cups tomato juice
1 teaspoon salt
1 1/2 teaspoons celery salt
Dash of pepper
2 teaspoons Worcestershire
  sauce
1/4 green pepper, chopped
1 3-ounce can sliced mushrooms (optional)
1 cup sour cream

Brown onion and ground beef in margarine. Add remaining ingredients, except sour cream.

Cook in large, heavy frypan on medium heat until noodles are tender. Add sour cream. Heat through.

Serves 8.

## Knobby Pines Goulash

**When our family of 14 gets together at the lake for a reunion,
a double recipe of goulash is one of our favorite
Saturday night meals.**

1 1/2 pounds ground beef
1 1/2 cups chopped celery
2 onions, chopped
2 beef bouillon cubes
1/2 cup hot water
1 10 1/2-ounce can tomato
    soup
1 16-ounce can stewed
    tomatoes
1 7-ounce package cooked
    Creamettes or egg
    noodles
Garlic salt, to taste
Onion salt, to taste
1 8-ounce can water chest-
    nuts, drained and sliced
    (optional)

Brown meat, celery and
onions. Drain. Dissolve
bouillon cubes in water. Add
soup, tomatoes, noodles and
seasoning. Pour into 2-quart
casserole.

Cover, and bake at 350° for
1 hour. Add water chestnuts
the last 1/2 hour of baking
time.

Serves 8 generously.

## Swedish Meatballs

**Freezes well.**

1 pound ground beef
1/2 cup fine bread crumbs
1 egg
2/3 cup milk
1/4 cup finely chopped
  onion
1/2 teaspoon salt
1/8 teaspoon pepper
1/4 teaspoon nutmeg
1 10 1/2-ounce can cream
  of mushroom soup

Combine all ingredients, except soup. Form into small balls.

Brown slowly. Pour off fat. Place in 1-quart casserole. Dilute soup with 1/4 cup water. Pour mixture over meatballs.

Bake at 325° for 1 hour, or 375° for 1/2 hour.

## Taco Pie

**This recipe may be doubled. Put in a 9-by-13-inch pan, and it will serve at least 10 people.**

1 can refrigerated crescent
  rolls
1 small or medium package
  taco chips, crushed
1 pound ground beef
1 8-ounce can tomato sauce
1/2 can (1/2 cup) water
1 package taco seasoning
1 cup sour cream
1 cup Mozzarella cheese,
  shredded

Brown the beef. Drain fat. Add tomato sauce, water and taco seasoning. Place crescent rolls in bottom of 10-inch pie plate. Layer other ingredients on top, in this order: 1/2 of crushed taco chips; ground beef mixture; sour cream; Mozzarella cheese; remaining taco chips.

Bake at 375° for 25 minutes.

Serves 6.

## Aunt Linnea's Five-Decker Dinner

**This entire meal is made in an electric frypan!**

6 slices of bacon, cut into
    1-inch pieces
1 pound ground beef, made
    into 4 patties
4 onions, sliced
4 medium potatoes, sliced
4 - 6 carrots, sliced
Salt and pepper to taste
1/4 cup chopped green
    pepper
1 tablespoon chopped
    parsley (optional)
1/4 cup water

Separate bacon squares, and place on bottom of frypan. Put ground beef patties on the bacon. Salt and pepper. Layer the onions, potatoes and carrots over this, seasoning with salt and pepper. Put green pepper and parsley on top.

Cook on medium heat until bacon is sizzling, 3 to 5 minutes. Add water. Cover. Turn heat to low. Cook about 45 minutes. Drain grease. Recipe can be increased; cook a little longer.

Serves 4.

# Texas Straw Hats

**Shredded cheese, sour cream and black olives can be served separately, allowing guests to add what they wish to the meat mixture.**

1 cup chopped onion
2/3 cup chopped celery
2/3 cup chopped green
    pepper
3 tablespoons oil
2 pounds ground beef
2 - 3 teaspoons chili powder
2 teaspoons salt
1/4 teaspoon pepper
2 6-ounce cans tomato paste
1/2 cup ketchup
2 cups water
2 teaspoons Worcestershire
    sauce
Dash Tabasco sauce
2 6-ounce packages
    corn chips
Shredded sharp American
    cheese

In large skillet, cook onions, celery and green pepper in oil until tender. Brown beef separately. Drain fat. Mix beef with onion, celery and green pepper. Add remaining ingredients, except chips and cheese.

Simmer, uncovered, for 1 hour, stirring occasionally. Serve on corn chips. Top generously with cheese. Keeps refrigerated for several days.

Serves 6.

# Salmon Loaf

1-pound can red salmon
1/4 cup shortening
1 teaspoon chopped onion
1 1/2 cups soft bread cubes
1 egg, slightly beaten
1/2 teaspoon salt
1/4 teaspoon black pepper
Salmon juice plus milk to
    make 1 cup
1 teaspoon lemon juice
1/4 teaspoon lemon rind
1 tablespoon fresh chopped
    parsley, or flakes

Flake salmon, removing large bones. Drain liquid, and add enough milk to make 1 cup. Melt shortening, and add onion. Cook until yellow. Add bread cubes and seasonings; brown. Add remaining ingredients.

Bake, uncovered, at 350° in glass loaf pan for about 45 minutes. Makes one loaf.

Serves 8.

# Beans and Wieners Supreme

**This dish is good served immediately, or can be re-heated. Keeps in refrigerator several days.**

1/4 pound bacon, diced
6 wieners, cut into 1-inch
    pieces
1/4 cup chopped onion
1/2 cup chopped green
    pepper
3/4 cup crushed or chunk
    pineapple, drained
1 31-ounce can pork and
    beans, drained
1/2 cup brown sugar,
    packed
1 cup ketchup
2 tablespoons Worcestershire
    sauce

Fry bacon until crisp. Add wieners, onion, pepper and pineapple. Cook and stir until onion is tender. Add remaining ingredients.

Cook over low heat for 1 hour, stirring occasionally, or bake, uncovered, at 300° for 1 hour.

Serves 8.

## Lake Dogs with Beans

1/2 cup butter
2 tablespoons prepared
    mustard
2 tablespoons Parmesan
    cheese
1 tablespoon finely chopped
    green pepper
1 tablespoon chopped onion
8 hot dog buns
8 frankfurters
1 16-ounce can pork and
    beans

Cream butter. Add mustard, cheese, green pepper and onion. Place buns on double-thick rectangles of foil. Spread mixture on both sides of split buns. Slit franks lengthwise, but do not cut through. Place franks on buns, and fill cavity with beans. Fold foil over sandwich.

Grill for 10 minutes on each side, or bake at 350° for 15 minutes.

Serves 8.

## Cabin Supper Special

### Popular with children.

8 wieners
1/4 cup Cheez Whiz (other
    cheese can be used)
1 - 2 tablespoons minced
    onion
2 cups mashed potatoes
    (instant is fine)
Paprika

Cook wieners, and set aside to cool somewhat. Melt cheese in top of double boiler, adding a small amount of milk to thin, if desired. Stir in minced onion. Add potatoes, and mix well. Split wieners lengthwise, and spoon potato-cheese mixture on top. Sprinkle with paprika.

Broil until lightly browned. Serves 4.

## Hash Brown Brunch or Supper

8 slices bacon
1 box dehydrated hash
    browns with onions
1 teaspoon salt
1 3/4 cups water
1/3 cup chopped green
    pepper
1 cup grated Cheddar
    cheese
4 large eggs
1/4 cup milk
1/2 teaspoon salt
Dash of pepper

Parboil pepper, and reserve water for the required water. Fry bacon in large electric skillet. Remove bacon, leaving 3 to 4 tablespoons bacon grease in skillet. Set temperature to 300°. Mix potatoes, salt, water and green pepper, and pour into skillet.

Cook, uncovered, until liquid is absorbed and bottom is golden brown, about 10 minutes. Turn. Reduce temperature to 250°. Sprinkle cheese over mixture. Mix eggs, milk, salt and pepper. Pour over cheese, and cover. Cook until eggs are done and potatoes are golden brown, about 12 minutes. Garnish with bacon.

Serves 6 generously.

# Ham Au Gratin

1/4 cup vegetable oil
1 pound frozen hash browns
1 pound ham, cut into bite-
sized pieces
1 cup plain yogurt, at room
temperature
1 10 1/2-ounce can Cheddar
cheese soup
1/2 teaspoon mustard

Heat oil, and brown hash browns (cover and cook 4 minutes; uncover and cook 8 minutes, or until golden). Put hash browns in buttered 9-inch-square baking pan. Cover with ham cubes. Combine yogurt, soup and mustard. Pour over casserole.

Bake at 400° for 20 to 25 minutes.

Serves 4 to 6.

# Chicken/Broccoli, Minnesota Style

1 chicken, cut up, or
chicken breasts
(3 1/2 pounds)
3 10-ounce packages frozen
broccoli
1 10 1/2-ounce can cream
of mushroom soup
2 10 1/2-ounce cans cream
of chicken soup
1 4 1/2-ounce can mush-
rooms, drained
Parmesan cheese

In a kettle, cook chicken with a small amount of water, until tender. Remove skin and bones. Cut chicken into small pieces. Cook broccoli until not quite done.

Alternate layers of chicken and broccoli in a 9-by-13-inch pan. In a bowl, mix the 3 cans of soup with 1 1/2 soup cans of water. Add drained mushrooms. Pour over chicken and broccoli. Sprinkle with Parmesan cheese.

Bake for 1 hour at 325°. Serves 10 to 12.

## Zucchini Crescent Pie

### MMMMMMMMMMM-good!

4 cups thinly sliced,
     unpeeled zucchini
1 cup coarsely chopped
     onion
1/2 cup margarine or butter
1/2 cup chopped parsley or
     2 tablespoons parsley
     flakes
1/2 teaspoon salt
1/4 teaspoon black pepper
1/4 teaspoon garlic powder
     (or salt)
1/4 teaspoon sweet basil
     leaves
1/4 teaspoon oregano leaves
2 eggs, well-beaten
8 ounces (2 cups) shredded
     Mozzarella cheese
1 8-ounce can refrigerated
     crescent dinner rolls
2 teaspoons Dijon prepared
     mustard

In a 10-inch skillet, cook zucchini and onion in margarine until tender—about 10 minutes. In a large bowl, combine parsley and seasonings. Blend in eggs and cheese. Stir in vegetable mixture.

Separate dough into 8 triangles. Place in ungreased 11-inch quiche pan or 10-inch pie pan. Press over bottom and up sides to form crust. Spread mustard onto crust. Pour vegetable mixture evenly into crust.

Bake at 375° (350° for glass dish) for 18 to 20 minutes.

Serves 6.

# Chicken and Stuffing Hot Dish

**A special treat for cabin guests.**

1 6-ounce box chicken-
flavored Stove Top
stuffing mix
1 10-ounce package frozen
broccoli spears
3 chicken breasts
1 10 1/2-ounce can cream
of chicken soup
1 cup grated Colby cheese

Prepare stuffing mix according to directions on the box. Slightly cook the broccoli spears. Cook the chicken breasts, and cut into bite-sized pieces. Mix the soup with 1 soup can water. Layer all ingredients, in order listed, in a 7 1/2-by-11 1/2-inch greased baking dish. Cover with foil.

Bake at 350° for 30 minutes.

Serves 8.

# Meat, Fish & Poultry

## Hamburger Stroganoff

**Serve over rice, buttered noodles, or boiled potatoes. If there are any leftovers, serve on toast for a quick lunch.**

**2 pounds hamburger, seasoned**
**2 medium onions**
**1 large can mushrooms, drained (reserve juice)**
**1 10 1/2-ounce can cream of mushroom soup**
**1 10 1/2-ounce can tomato soup**
**1 pint sour cream**

Brown hamburger. Drain fat. Saute onions in mushroom juice, and drain. Mix all ingredients. Simmer. Can re-heat over low heat when needed.

Serves 8 to 10.

## Make-Ahead Hamburgers

**Do your own thing! Recipe is not explicit, but the burgers will be good.**

**Hamburger patties**
**Barbecue sauce**

Using your favorite hamburger or meatloaf recipe, shape mixture into hamburger patties.

Fry. (At this point, the hamburgers may be refrigerated or frozen.) Place hamburgers in a baking dish or roaster. Pour barbecue sauce over them. Cover.

Heat in oven. Serve on buns.

## Pot Roast Supreme

**Tender and delicious. Works well with less expensive cuts of beef.**

1 beef roast (about
   3 pounds)
Flour
6 carrots, peeled
6 potatoes, peeled
1 10 1/2-ounce can onion
   soup, heated

Dredge meat with flour on both sides. Brown the roast. No seasoning necessary. Add carrots and potatoes to roast. Pour heated soup over all.

Bake, covered, at 275° for 4 hours.

Serves 6.

## Beef Brisket

**This is tasty and tender.**

3 - 4 pounds beef brisket,
   rinsed and patted dry
3 tablespoons brown (apple
   cider) vinegar
Accent
Lawry's seasoned salt
Lots of paprika
Garlic salt
1 onion, sliced

Sprinkle all ingredients on top of meat.

Bake, uncovered, at 350° for 1 hour. Add 2 cups hot water. Cover.

Bake 3 to 4 hours longer. Slice thin and serve.

Serves 10 to 12.

# Barbecued Beef Brisket

**This can be started a few days before serving.**

**6 pounds beef brisket**
**Garlic, onion and celery salt**
**3 tablespoons liquid smoke**
**Salt and pepper**
**Worcestershire sauce**
**18-ounce bottle barbecue**
   **sauce**

Sprinkle all sides of brisket with flavored salts. Place brisket in glass dish. Pour liquid smoke on meat. Cover, and refrigerate overnight. Before baking, sprinkle meat with flavored salts, salt, pepper and Worcestershire sauce.

Bake, covered, at 250° for 5 hours. (May be done ahead to this point and refrigerated for later re-heating.) Slice thin. Add barbecue sauce. Bake at 250° for 1 1/2 hours. May thicken sauce with flour.

Serves 12 to 15.

# Salisbury Steak

**2 pounds ground beef**
**1/2 cup bread crumbs**
**2/3 cup beef bouillon**
**2 teaspoons instant**
   **chopped onions**
**1 egg**
**2 teaspoons salt**

Mix all ingredients well. Portion and shape into 8 steaks.

Bake at 350° for 10 to 15 minutes.

## Grilled Flank Steak

**Put meat in marinade at home, and take to destination in a plastic bag in your cooler. Good with baked potatoes and cole slaw.**

**1 1/2 - 2 pounds flank steak**
**1/4 cup soy sauce**
**3 tablespoons honey**
**1/2 teaspoon ginger**
**1/2 cup salad oil**
**2 tablespoons vinegar**
**1/2 teaspoon garlic powder**

Lightly score flank steak against the grain. Marinate in the rest of the ingredients for 24 to 48 hours. Keep in a covered glass pan or in a plastic bag in a bowl or pan in the refrigerator.

Grill for 5 to 7 minutes per side. Slice thin, across the grain.

Serves about 3 people per pound of meat.

## Pork Tenderloin Stacks

**4 slices pork tenderloin or**
    **pork chops**
**4 slices sweet onion**
**4 slices tomato**
**4 slices American cheese**
**2 slices bacon, cut in half**

Brown the tenderloin slices, seasoning to taste. Stack on remaining ingredients, in order listed, skewering together with a toothpick. Place in pan or casserole. Cover.

Bake at 350° for 1 1/2 hours. Uncover after 1 hour, so bacon will become crisp.

Serves 4.

## Cheese-Stuffed Patties

1 pound ground beef
1/2 teaspoon salt
Dash pepper
American cheese, shredded
Chopped onion
Bottled barbecue sauce

Mix ground beef, salt and pepper. Divide meat into 6 portions, and pat out 1/4-inch-thick between sheets of waxed paper. Place small amount of cheese, onion and barbecue sauce in centers of 3 patties. Top with remaining meat patties. Press around edges to seal.

Grill over medium-hot coals for about 7 minutes on each side, or broil.

Makes 3 burgers.


## Liver and Vegetables, Pennsylvania Dutch Style

**Aunt Gladys recommends this for all liver lovers.**

1 pound beef liver, cut into
    serving pieces
1 small onion, sliced
4 potatoes, quartered
4 carrots, split lengthwise
Salt and pepper to taste
1 cup water
Flour

Dip liver into flour. Brown both sides in heavy frying pan or electric skillet (with tight-fitting lid). Add onions, potatoes and carrots. Pour water over ingredients. Cover tightly.

Simmer for 1 hour, or until carrots and potatoes are done.

Serves 4 to 5.

## Florida Pork Chops

4 pork chops or 2 pork
   steaks (do not
   pre-brown
1 cup orange juice
1/4 cup brown sugar
1 teaspoon salt
1 teaspoon dry mustard
1/4 teaspoon pepper (lemon
   pepper or fresh-ground
   is best)

Place pork chops in an
8-inch-square baking dish.
Mix remaining ingredients.
Pour over top of chops. Add
additional orange juice, if
needed, to cover.

Bake at 350° for 1 1/4
hours.

Serves 2 or 4.

## Hinds Lake Fish with Sesame Butter

2 pounds northern pike
   or walleye
1/2 cup butter, melted
4 tablespoons lemon juice
Dash Worcestershire sauce
6 tablespoons toasted sesame
   seeds
Salt and pepper
Lemon quarters
Parsley

Arrange fish in well-buttered,
shallow baking dish. Season
with salt and pepper. Brush
with some of the melted
butter.

Bake at 350° for 20 minutes,
or until fish flakes easily
when tested with a fork.

Heat remaining butter until
very lightly brown. Add
lemon juice and Worcestershire sauce. Stir in sesame
seeds. Spoon over baked fish.
Serve with lemon quarters
and parsley.

# Joe's Crappies

## This one is hard to beat.

Crappies
Soda crackers
Flour
Margarine
Vegetable oil

Salt both sides of fillets, and let them rest awhile. Crush soda crackers, and put into a plastic bag. Add some flour to bag of crumbs, if desired. Heat frying pan with half margarine and half vegetable oil. Drop fillets into plastic bag, and shake well.

Fry fillets quickly until tender. Place on paper toweling to drain. If fillets cannot be cooked within 24 hours, freeze in plastic containers of water.

# Fish Fillets Almondine

## Serve your catch for dinner tonight.

Fish fillets, fresh or frozen, thawed (walleye, northern pike or bass)
2 tablespoons butter or margarine per fillet
1 teaspoon lemon juice per fillet
Paprika
Lemon pepper
Bread crumbs, very fine
Almonds, slivers or slices

Arrange fillets in 9-by-9-inch baking dish. Melt butter. Add lemon juice. Pour over fillets. Cover the fillets completely. Sprinkle with paprika, lemon pepper and bread crumbs.

Bake at 450° for 8 to 15 minutes, or until fish flakes easily. Add almonds the last 2 minutes. Watch carefully. Serves 4.

## Northern Pike, Swedish Style

Clean the fish by slitting the underside, scaling and removing the innards. Place fish in a large pan, and cover half-way with water. Add peppercorns, a bay leaf and a sliced onion. Bring to a boil.

Boil gently for 10 minutes. With spatulas, carefully turn fish over, and cook for another 10 minutes. Remove fish, and arrange in a curved shape on a plate. Peel back the skin. Serve with one or more of the following garnishes: melted butter, horseradish, or grated hard-cooked eggs.

## Honey-Fried Walleye Fillets

**6 large walleye fillets**
**2/3 cup vegetable oil**
**1 egg, lightly beaten**
**1 teaspoon honey**
**1 1/2 cups coarsely crushed
    soda crackers**
**1/2 cup flour**
**1/2 teaspoon salt**
**1/2 teaspoon pepper**

Dry fillets on paper towel. Heat oil in a 10-inch skillet. Combine and mix the egg and honey. Dip fillets into the mixture. Then, coat with a mixture of cracker crumbs, flour, salt and pepper, pressing crumbs firmly into fillets.

Fry about 3 minutes on each side in preheated oil.

Serves 6.

## Easy Baked Fish

**Celery soup provides a new taste in this fish recipe.**

12 - 14 cleaned panfish,
    fresh or frozen
1/3 cup butter or margarine
1 10 1/2-ounce can cream of
    celery soup
1/2 cup lemon juice
1/4 cup parsley flakes,
    dehydrated

Melt butter in 9-by-13-inch pan. Arrange fish in butter. Pour other ingredients, in order listed, over fish.

Bake at 350° for 50 minutes, or until fish flakes easily.

Serves 6.

## Caesar's Fillets

**Attention all microwave owners—try this recipe with your next catch.**

1 pound fish fillets
1/2 cup Caesar salad dressing
1/2 cup seasoned bread
    crumbs
1/2 cup shredded Cheddar
    cheese

Dry fish fillets well. Moisten thoroughly with Caesar dressing. Lay single layer in a microwave pan. Cover with bread crumbs. Top with Cheddar cheese. Cover.

Microwave on high until fish flakes easily with a fork, or until cheese is melted. Check after 5 minutes. Let stand a minute. Check again.

Serves 2 to 3.

## Sweet and Sour Chicken Wings

These tasty chicken wings may be used as an appetizer, or for a light meal. Delicious served hot or cold. Bake at home, and take to your destination in the cooler—will keep for several days.

20 to 25 chicken wings
1 cup soy sauce
1 cup pineapple juice
1 teaspoon garlic powder
1 cup water
1 cup sugar
1/4 cup salad oil
1 teaspoon ground ginger

Cut each wing in half. Discard tips. Combine all ingredients. Pour over wings in shallow baking pan. Refrigerate at least 1 hour, but overnight is better. Remove wings from sauce and place on baking sheet.

Bake, uncovered, at 350° for 1 to 1 1/4 hours, or until brown and tender.

## Glazed Chicken

### Easy and tasty!

1 fryer chicken, cut up,
    or 4 chicken breasts
    with skin on
8-ounce bottle Russian
    dressing
1 cup apricot preserves
    (or orange marmalade)
1 package dry onion soup

Combine dressing, preserves and dry soup. Pour over chicken in baking dish.

Bake, uncovered, at 350° for 1 to 1 1/2 hours, or until fork-tender. Baste occasionally while baking.

# Tarragon Chicken

### This is good, hot or cold.

**2 broiler-fryer chickens, cut into serving pieces**
**1/2 cup melted butter or margarine**
**Salt**
**Pepper**
**Paprika**
**Chili powder**
**Dried tarragon**

Melt butter or margarine in shallow baking pan. Place chicken, skin side down, in pan. Sprinkle with salt, pepper, paprika, chili powder and 1 teaspoon tarragon.

Place under broiler, about 5 inches from heat. Broil for about 15 minutes. Turn pieces over, repeat sprinkling of seasonings. Broil again for 15 minutes. Remove from broiler, and cover pan tightly with foil.

Bake at 325° for 25 to 30 minutes.

Serves 5 to 6.

# Honey Chicken

**Good with rice, peas, and a green salad containing mandarin orange slices.**

3 pounds chicken, cut up
4 tablespoons butter
1/2 cup honey
1/4 cup prepared mustard
1 teaspoon salt
1 teaspoon curry powder

Wash and dry chicken. Remove skin, if desired. Melt butter, and mix in remaining ingredients. Roll chicken in mixture to coat. Arrange meaty side up in a single layer. Cover with remaining sauce.

Bake at 375° for 1 hour, or until chicken is tender and glazed.

# Chinese Chicken

**Delish!**

1/3 cup soy sauce
2 tablespoons oil
1 teaspoon dry mustard
1/2 teaspoon ginger
1/4 teaspoon pepper
1 clove garlic, minced
1 fryer, cut up

Combine first 6 ingredients. Brush over washed and drained chicken parts. Let stand 1/2 hour, and again brush with sauce. Put in shallow pan, or on rack if crisp chicken is desired.

Bake in 375° oven for about 50 minutes. Brush with sauce every 15 minutes.

Drippings may be used as gravy on potatoes or biscuits. Sauce may be made ahead of time and stored in a jar.

# Parmesan Chicken

**Delicious hot or cold. Easy to make ahead of time.**

2 chickens, skinned and
   cut up
1 cup butter, melted
2 cups Italian bread crumbs
1 cup grated Parmesan cheese
1/4 teaspoon instant minced
   garlic
1/2 teaspoon, or more, salt
2 tablespoons parsley flakes

Melt butter in pan. Combine bread crumbs, Parmesan cheese, garlic, salt and parsley flakes. Dip chicken pieces into butter. Roll in crumb mixture. Arrange in pan.

Bake, uncovered, at 375° for 1 hour.

Serves 6 to 8.

# Delicious Easy Chicken

**Chicken can be assembled, covered and refrigerated the night before baking. Bake as directed.**

6 to 8 chicken breasts, split
   and deboned
1 10 1/2-ounce can cream of
   mushroom soup
1/2 cup sour cream
1/4 cup Hellmann's
   mayonnaise
1/4 cup dry white Vermouth

Combine soup, sour cream, mayonnaise and Vermouth. Pour over chicken breasts, which have been rolled and placed seam side down in greased casserole or 9-by-13-inch pan.

Bake, uncovered, at 250° for 2 1/2 to 3 hours. Wild or white rice would be a good accompaniment.

Serves 6 to 8.

## Breast of Chicken on Rice

1 10 1/2-ounce can cream of
    mushroom soup
1 soup can milk
3/4 cup uncooked white rice
    (1/2 of this can be
    wild rice)
1 4-ounce can mushroom
    stems and pieces, plus
    liquid
1 envelope onion soup mix
3 chicken breasts, boneless,
    cut in half (or a 2 1/2-
    pound chicken, cut up)

Mix the mushroom soup with milk. Reserve 1/2 cup of this mixture for later use. Combine soup mixture with the rice, mushrooms and liquid and 1/2 of the onion soup mix. Pour into an oblong baking dish or 7 1/2-by-11 1/2-inch pan. Place breasts on top. Pour the reserved soup mixture over the chicken breasts. Sprinkle with the rest of the onion soup mix. Cover.

Bake at 350° for 1 hour. Uncover, and bake 15 minutes longer.

Serves 6.

## Crock Pot Goose or Duck

**Our family jokes: If the goose is not tender after 6 or 7 hours of cooking, add 1 quart of red wine. Cook 1 hour longer. Discard the goose and drink the juice!**

1 duck or goose, cut up
1 teaspoon Morton's
   seasoning salt
Lawry's seasoning salt
Accent
2 oranges, quartered
2 apples, quartered
2 stalks celery, chopped
2 carrots, chopped
1 onion, chopped

Put 3 cups water in crock pot. Add Morton's seasoning. Sprinkle Lawry's and/or Accent on meat pieces. Put meat into crock pot.

Cook on high for at least 2 hours (longer if game is frozen). Turn to low. Continue cooking for 4 to 5 hours, or until done. Discard vegetables. Serve with orange sauce. (See page 203.)

# Vegetables & Side Dishes

## Dilly Beans

**This relish will keep in the refrigerator for several weeks.**

**Fresh green beans**
**1/2 cup white vinegar**
**1/2 cup water**
**1/4 - 1/2 cup sugar**
**1 teaspoon dry dill weed,**
**    or 3 heads fresh dill**

Wash the beans, and cut off ends. Cut into pieces, if desired. Boil in unsalted water for 3 to 5 minutes, until just tender. Blanch in ice water.

Mix vinegar, water, sugar and dill weed. Pour over beans. Store in covered container in the refrigerator.

## German Green Beans

**1 can (about 1 pound)**
**    green beans, mostly**
**    drained**
**2 slices bacon, cut up**
**1 green onion, cut up**
**    (or onion salt)**
**1 tablespoon vinegar**
**Parmesan cheese**

Fry bacon. Add beans to bacon and grease. Add onion and vinegar. Heat thoroughly. Put in serving bowl, sprinkle with Parmesan cheese.

Serves 3 to 4.

## Bestemor's Baked Beans for a Crowd

**Delicious! Recipe may easily be cut in half.**

6 16-ounce cans Bush's
    baked beans
1 1/2 pounds ground beef
1 pound bacon, cut into
    small pieces
3 4-ounce cans mushrooms,
    drained
1 1/2 cups ketchup
1 cup brown sugar
2 teaspoons dry mustard

Brown the ground beef. Fry bacon. Drain fat. Combine all ingredients.

Bake at 325 ° until thoroughly heated—about 1 hour. Can also be heated in a crockpot, for 4 hours or longer.

Serves 18 to 20.

## Easy Baked Beans

2 1-pound cans baked beans
    in tomato sauce
1 teaspoon dry mustard
3/4 cup brown sugar
1/2 cup ketchup
6 slices bacon, cut up

Mix mustard and brown sugar. Layer the beans and the sugar mixture in baking dish. Pour ketchup over the top. Sprinkle with bacon pieces.

Bake at 325 ° for 3 hours.

Serves 6 to 8.

## Broccoli Supreme

1 20-ounce bag frozen
   chopped broccoli
1 10 1/2-ounce can cream
   of chicken soup
2 carrots, grated
1/2 cup (4 ounces) sour
   cream
1/2 2.8-ounce can French
   fried onions or croutons

Cook broccoli according to package instructions. Drain. Mix with soup, carrots, sour cream and fried onions. Turn into lightly greased medium-sized casserole.

Bake at 350° for 30 minutes.

Serves 6 to 8.

## Baked Corn

1 16-ounce can cream style
   corn
1 16-ounce can whole kernel
   corn, drained
1 egg, beaten
1/2 cup bread or cracker
   crumbs
1/2 cup sour cream
1/2 teaspoon salt
Dash of pepper

Combine all ingredients. Mix well. Put in buttered casserole.

Bake at 350° for about 40 minutes, or until firm.

Serves 6.

# Hot Fruit Compote

### A colorful addition to any meal. Excellent!

1 16-ounce can apricots,
  quartered
1 16-ounce can sliced
  peaches
1 15 1/4-ounce can
  pineapple chunks
1 14-ounce jar apple rings,
  quartered
1 16-ounce can pear halves,
  quartered
2 tablespoons flour
1/2 cup sugar
1/2 cup butter
1 cup golden sherry

Drain fruit, and arrange in large casserole or 9-by-13-inch baking dish. Heat butter, sugar and flour until thick as cream. Add sherry. Pour over fruit, and let stand in refrigerator at least 8 hours or up to 24 hours.

Bake, covered, at 350° for 25 minutes and uncovered for 5 to 10 minutes. Serve immediately. Keeps up to one week in refrigerator.

# Cucumber Sidecar

### Excellent with fish.

2 or 3 cucumbers, peeled
  and sliced
1 small onion, chopped
2 heaping tablespoons
  mayonnaise or salad
  dressing
2 tablespoons sugar
1/2 teaspoon celery seed
Salt and pepper to taste

Combine cucumbers and onion. Add remaining ingredients. Stir into vegetables. Can make about 1 hour before mealtime.

## Scandinavian Cucumbers

1/2 cup sour cream
1 tablespoon sugar
2 tablespoons snipped
    parsley
2 tablespoons tarragon
    vinegar
1 tablespoon finely chopped
    onion
1/4 teaspoon dried dill weed
2 or 3 small cucumbers,
    thinly sliced

Mix all ingredients, except cucumbers. Fold mixture into cucumbers.

Cover, and chill for 2 hours.

## Cucumber Relish

8 cucumbers, peeled and
    sliced as thin as
    possible
1 onion, sliced very thin
1 cup vinegar
1 1/2 cups sugar
2 tablespoons salt

Combine vinegar, sugar and salt. Pour over cucumbers and onions. Refrigerate overnight before serving. Keeps well up to 20 days, when refrigerated.

## Carrots and Celery, Simply Together

**Colorful, tasty and low-cal! You decide how much to serve, and prepare accordingly.**

Sliced carrots
Sliced celery
Instant chicken bouillon
    granules

Bring water—enough so that it covers vegetables—to a boil. Add about 1 teaspoon bouillon granules for each cup of water. Add vegetables. Simmer just until tender.

## Cauliflower and Carrots

1 small head cauliflower,
    broken into small pieces
2 - 3 carrots, sliced
1 10 1/2-ounce can cream of
    chicken soup, undiluted
2 cups grated Cheddar
    cheese
1 cup bread crumbs

Cook cauliflower and carrots, until just tender. In a greased, 2-quart casserole, layer half of vegetables, soup and cheese. Repeat layering. Cover top with bread crumbs.

Bake at 350° for 30 minutes, or until bubbly.

Cream of celery or mushroom soup may be used as a substitute.

Serves 6.

## Carrot-Cheese-Rice Casserole

2 cups cooked rice
2 1/2 cups grated carrots
1/3 pound grated Colby or
    Cheddar cheese
2 eggs, beaten
1/4 cup milk
1 tablespoon butter,
    softened
1/4 cup chopped onion
1 teaspoon salt
1/8 teaspoon pepper

Mix all ingredients. Pour into a 1 1/2-quart casserole.

Bake at 350° for 45 minutes to 1 hour, or until carrots are done.

Serves 6.

# Carrots with Apples and Honey

**A surprisingly tasty combination.**

**1 pound (2 cups) carrots**
**1 teaspoon salt**
**2/3 cup honey**
**1 3/4 cups diced apples**
**1 teaspoon lemon juice**

Scrape carrots, split into halves, and slice about 1/4-inch thick. Place carrots in saucepan, and cover with water.

Boil gently until tender. Drain liquid. Add salt, lemon juice and honey to 2 table-spoons drained liquid. Add diced apples.

Simmer gently for about 10 minutes. Add carrots. Simmer until apples are tender, about 5 minutes.

Serves 4 to 6.

# Savory Grilled Onions

**May be prepared in advance and cooked at your picnic site.**

**1 medium-to-large onion**
**per person**
**Granulated beef bouillon**

Peel and core onion. Set onion on 12-inch square of aluminum foil. Fill center of onion with bouillon. Seal edges of foil.

Place on charcoal grill for 30 to 45 minutes, turning occasionally.

# Granny's Grits

**Margaret and Jack's favorite from the ol' South.**

1 cup quick-cooking grits
4 cups water
1 1/2 teaspoons salt
1/2 cup margarine
1 cup Longhorn cheese, grated
4 eggs
1 cup milk
Pepper

Cook grits, water and salt according to directions on the grits package. Add margarine and 3/4 cup cheese to grits. Let cook slightly. Add lightly beaten eggs, milk and pepper. Stir until well-mixed. Pour into 1 1/2-quart casserole. Top with remaining cheese.

Bake at 350° for 1 hour.

Serves 6.

# Fried Green Tomatoes

**Can't wait until your tomatoes ripen? Try these.**

1/2 cup flour
4 medium green tomatoes, cut into thick slices
4 tablespoons bacon grease, or oil

Dredge each side of tomato slices with flour. Fry in hot grease, turning to brown both sides. Sprinkle with salt and pepper.

## Dilled Peas

### Dill-icious!

1/4 cup water
2 beef bouillon cubes
3 tablespoons butter
1 teaspoon finely chopped
    onion
1/4 teaspoon dill weed
Pepper
2 10-ounce packages frozen
    peas

Bring water to a boil. Blend in beef cubes, butter, onion, dill and pepper. Add peas. Return to boil.

Simmer until tender, about 5 minutes.

Serves 6.

## Peas To Please

1/3 cup butter or margarine
3 or 4 whole green onions
1 box frozen peas

Melt butter in heavy saucepan. Place green onions, tops and all, in saucepan. Add frozen peas. Do not add water.

Cook *slowly* until peas are crispy-tender, about 15 to 20 minutes. Season with salt and pepper. Discard onions, and serve.

## Zucchini Casserole

### You'll be asked for this recipe!

3 pounds zucchini
3 onions, chopped
1 stick butter
1/2 pound fresh mushrooms
   (canned mushrooms
   are OK)

*Sauce:*
2 tablespoons butter, melted
1/2 cup grated Cheddar
   cheese
1 teaspoon seasoned salt
1 cup sour cream

*Topping:*
2 tablespoons grated
   Cheddar cheese
Crushed Ritz crackers

Slice zucchini into thin slices. Parboil in salted water, uncovered. Drain. Saute onions in butter. Add mushrooms, and saute.

Add cheese, seasoned salt and sour cream to melted butter. Mix with vegetables, and heat through. Pour into 1 1/2- or 2-quart casserole.

Sprinkle topping over all.

Bake, uncovered, at 350° for 30 minutes.

Serves 8.

## Rice Casserole

### A good side dish that freezes well.

1 cup raw rice
1 10-ounce package chopped
   broccoli
4 tablespoons margarine
1 small onion, chopped
1/2 cup chopped celery
1 10 1/2-ounce can cream
   of chicken soup
1 8-ounce jar Cheez Whiz

Cook rice with no salt. Cook broccoli until tender, and drain. Fry onion and celery in margarine until tender. Combine rice, broccoli, soup, Cheez Whiz, onion and celery.

Bake at 350° for 30 minutes. Serves 6.

## Easy Rice Casserole

**This is a delicious accompaniment to beef. A double recipe fits nicely into a crockpot. Rice can be re-heated in a crockpot for serving.**

1 1/2 cups converted rice, uncooked
1 10 1/2-ounce can beef consomme
1 10 1/2-ounce can onion soup
8 ounces canned mushrooms and juice
1/4 pound butter
1/3 cup Parmesan cheese

Combine and mix all ingredients.

Bake, uncovered, at 350° for 1 hour. Stir occasionally. For a double recipe, bake about 1 hour and 25 minutes, or until rice is absorbed. Can also prepare by cooking in a covered crockpot for 5 to 6 hours.

## Noodles and Rice Casserole

1/2 cup margarine
1/2 pound fine egg noodles
2 cups uncooked minute rice
2 10 1/2-ounce cans Campbell's onion broth or soup
2 10 1/2-ounce cans chicken broth
4 tablespoons soy sauce
1 8-ounce can water chestnuts, sliced
1 4-ounce can mushroom pieces (optional)

Melt margarine in large skillet. Add uncooked noodles. Cook until brown, stirring constantly. Add uncooked rice and remaining ingredients. Mix well. Put in 3-quart casserole.

Bake, uncovered, at 350° for 45 minutes, stirring occasionally.

Serves 10 to 12.

## Wild Rice Casserole

1 cup wild rice, raw
1/2 onion, chopped
2 tablespoons butter or
    margarine
3 chicken bouillon cubes
1/4 cup hot water
1 10 1/2-ounce can cream
    of mushroom soup
1 soup can water
2 3 1/2-ounce cans mush-
    rooms, drained, or
    fresh mushrooms

Wash and drain the rice. Saute onion in butter or margarine. Dissolve chicken bouillon cubes in 1/4 cup hot water. Combine all ingredients in casserole.

Bake at 325° for 1 1/2 to 2 hours. Do not overcook. This may accompany a main meat dish, or 1/4 to 1 pound of ground beef (browned) may be added. Freezes well.

Serves 6 to 8.

## Rice and Fresh Mushrooms

1/2 cup butter, melted
1 1/2 cups raw rice
1 10 1/2-ounce can beef
    consomme
1 10 1/2-ounce can onion
    soup
1/2 pound fresh mushrooms,
    sliced
8 ounces (2 cups) shredded
    sharp Cheddar cheese

Melt butter in 1 1/2-quart pan. Add rice, soups and mushrooms. Pour into 11-by-7-by-1-inch baking dish.

Bake at 350° for about 1 hour. Sprinkle with cheese for the last few minutes of baking.

## Sweet/Sour Vegetables

**Double the recipe, and carry to the lake in an ice cream pail.**

1/2 bunch broccoli, cut into
    bite-sized pieces
1/2 head cauliflower, cut
    into small flowerettes
2 carrots, sliced
2 zucchini (cucumber-sized),
    sliced
1 large mild onion, sliced

*Dressing:*
1 1/2 cups cider vinegar,
    heated
1/3 cup sugar
1/4 cup salad oil
1 teaspoon salt

Mix dressing ingredients.
Pour over vegetables. Toss.
Cover, and chill overnight.
Good for several days in the
refrigerator.

Add button mushrooms and
ripe olives to dress it up for
company.

Serves 6 to 8.

## Sliced Baked Potatoes

**Easy and popular.**

Baking potatoes (1 per
    person)
Butter (about 4 tablespoons
    for a 9-by-13-inch pan)
Parmesan cheese (optional)

Peel potatoes. Slice lengthwise into 1/4-inch-thick
slices. Melt butter in pan in
oven. Put potatoes in pan,
and turn them over, coating
both sides with the butter.

Bake at 400° for 30 minutes,
or 350° for 40 minutes.
Sprinkle with salt before serving. Can also sprinkle with
Parmesan cheese.

## Sunshine Lemon Potatoes

**Great with fish. Different, very good and easy!**

1/4 cup melted butter
1 tablespoon freshly
    squeezed lemon juice
3 large potatoes, thinly
    sliced
2 teaspoons freshly grated
    lemon peel
3 tablespoons Parmesan
    cheese (can substitute
    seasoned croutons)
1/2 teaspoon paprika

Arrange potatoes in 9-by-13-inch baking dish. Combine butter and lemon juice. Brush over potatoes. Combine lemon peel, cheese and paprika. Sprinkle over potatoes.

Bake at 350° for 45 minutes.

Serves 4.

## Scalloped Potatoes

**This recipe does not have precise amounts. It's one of those wonderful dishes that you can prepare for any number of people. Somehow, the whipping cream and water combination will not curdle or become watery.**

Sliced raw potatoes
Whipping cream
Salt and pepper
Parmesan cheese (optional)

Layer potatoes in baking dish, sprinkling salt and pepper on them rather generously. Using equal parts of whipping cream and water, pour over potatoes, covering about 2/3 depth of potatoes. Sprinkle with Parmesan cheese.

Bake, uncovered, at 350° for about 1 hour, or until done.

## Mashed Potato Casserole

**Put together at home, and bake at the lake. Mash your potatoes in advance, without the last-minute fuss.**

5 pounds red potatoes,
    peeled and cooked
1 8-ounce package cream
    cheese, softened
1 cup Half and Half
1/2 cup butter, melted
1 teaspoon salt
1 teaspoon onion salt
1/4 teaspoon paprika

Combine cream cheese with Half and Half, beating until well-blended. Add well-drained potatoes. Mash, blending well. Add salt, onion salt and all but 1 tablespoon of the melted butter. Put into a 2-quart casserole. Brush with the tablespoon of butter. Sprinkle with paprika.

If baking immediately, bake at 350° for 30 minutes. If refrigerated for later baking, bake at 350° for 45 minutes.

Serves 12 to 15.

## Potato Casserole

3 cups Half and Half
1 cup skim milk
1/2 cup butter, melted
2/3 cup Parmesan cheese
1 teaspoon salt
2 pounds Ore Ida
    southern style frozen
    hash browns

Combine Half and Half, milk and cooled butter in 2-quart glass casserole. Add cheese, salt and hash browns.

Bake, covered, at 325° for 45 minutes. Remove cover. Bake 15 minutes more.

Serves 6 to 8.

## Vermicelli in a Frypan

### An excellent meat accompaniment.

1/2 pound butter
1 1/2 7-ounce packages
    vermicelli
1 cup dry Minute Rice
2 10 1/2-ounce cans onion
    soup
1 cup sliced mushrooms
4 green onions, chopped
    (include tops)

Melt butter in a large frypan. Add dry (uncooked) vermicelli, and fry until brown. Add dry rice, and brown a little longer. Add soup and enough water to make a total of 3 cups of liquid.

Cover, and simmer for 20 minutes. Stir, and add mushrooms and green onions. Cover, and cook another 20 minutes. Add more water if necessary.

Serves 8.

## Fried Apple Rings

### A tasty accompaniment to ham, sausage or pork.

Tart apples
Butter
Brown sugar or
    grated cheese

Core the apples. Peel only if the skins are tough. Slice into 1/2-inch rings.

Saute in butter, until barely tender. Turn over. When apples are nearly tender, sprinkle lightly with brown sugar or grated cheese. Cover, and cook until the sugar or cheese melts.

# Desserts

# Red Grape Dessert

### For dessert, or snack, or brunch, or . . .

**1 pound seedless red grapes**
**1/4 cup sour cream**
**1/4 cup cream cheese,**
**softened**
**2 tablespoons sugar**

Combine sour cream, cream cheese and sugar. Fold into grapes. Refrigerate for a few hours before serving. Keeps well for a few days in the refrigerator. Serve in small bowls.

Serves 4 to 6.

# Fresh Fruit Compote

### Can be used at any meal.

**Fresh fruit, a variety**
**Sugar**
**1/4 cup orange liqueur or**
**kirsch (optional)**

Prepare a variety of fresh, seasonal fruit. Arrange in layers in a glass bowl, sprinkling sugar lightly over each layer. Spoon liqueur over each layer for flavor, if you choose. Toss gently, and chill for 2 or more hours.

Some suggested fruits: peaches, nectarines, blue- berries, strawberries, canta- loupe, honeydew, grapes, watermelon.

## Cantaloupe with Blueberry Yogurt

### Pretty!

Cut cantaloupe into wedges. Top each wedge with a generous dollop of blueberry yogurt.

## Frozen Grapes

### A frosty treat for a hot summer day. Appreciated by dieters.

**Green or red seedless grapes**

Wash grapes, and remove stems. Drain on paper toweling. Freeze in a single layer. When frozen, transfer to plastic bag or other container. Eat, and enjoy.

## Orange Strawberry Dessert

**1 6-ounce can frozen orange juice concentrate, thawed**
**3/4 cup sugar**
**1 pint strawberries, washed, hulled and halved**
**6 oranges, peeled and sectioned**

Mix thawed concentrate and sugar. Let stand several minutes, until sugar is dissolved. Combine strawberries and orange sections. Pour concentrate mixture over fruit. Mix well. Refrigerate several hours or overnight.

Serves 6.

## Heavenly Summer Fruit Delight

Raspberries, blueberries,
strawberries, peaches, or
whatever fruit you like
Sour cream
Brown sugar

Spoon a dollop of cold sour cream (about 1 heaping table-spoon per serving) on top of cold, clean fruit. Sprinkle generously with brown sugar.

## Frozen Fruit Cup

**Versatile! This can be a breakfast fruit, a lunch dessert, or a dinner salad. Great to have on hand for unexpected guests.**

2 10-ounce packages frozen
strawberries, thawed
1 16-ounce can apricots,
drained and cut up
1 20-ounce can crushed
pineapple, not drained
4 bananas, diced

*Syrup:*
2 cups sugar
1 cup water

Mix fruit.

Bring sugar and water to a boil. Cool. Pour over the mixed fruit. Ladle into individual serving dishes. Freeze. Cover with foil when frozen. Remove from freezer 35 to 45 minutes before serv-ing. Paper souffle cups, or 5-ounce plastic glasses, make good serving dishes.

Makes 15 to 25 individual servings, depending upon size of serving dish.

## Blueberry-Green Grape Combo

2 cups blueberries
2 cups green grapes
3/4 cup sour cream
1/4 cup brown sugar

Combine sour cream and brown sugar. Toss with fruit. Put into 4 serving dishes. Sprinkle with brown sugar for garnish. Chill before serving.

Serves 4.

## Orange Take-Along Cake

1 1/4 cups boiling water
1 cup quick-cooking oats
1/2 cup butter or margarine, softened
1 cup granulated sugar
1/2 cup brown sugar
2 eggs
1/2 cup frozen orange juice concentrate, thawed and undiluted
1 teaspoon vanilla
1 3/4 cups flour
1 teaspoon baking powder
1 teaspoon baking soda
1/2 teaspoon salt
1/2 teaspoon cinnamon
1/2 cup walnuts

Pour boiling water over oats. Set aside. Cream butter and sugars. Beat in eggs, one at a time. Add orange juice and vanilla. Sift dry ingredients. Blend into creamed mixture alternately with oats, beginning and ending with flour mixture. Fold in nuts. Pour into greased 9-by-13-inch pan.

Bake at 350° for 40 minutes.

## Summer Fruit Favorite

1/2 pound (4 cups) Natural
   100 cereal, or any plain
   granola cereal
1/4 cup melted butter
2 cups sugar
3/4 cup soft butter
2 eggs, beaten
Fresh strawberries, about
   1 quart, cleaned and
   sliced
3 - 4 sliced bananas
1 pint whipping cream

Blend cereal in blender. Reserve some crumbs (1/3 cup) for top. Combine cereal and melted butter. Pat into 9-by-13-inch pan. Chill.

Cream sugar and soft butter. Add eggs, and blend. Pour into pan. Cover with strawberries and bananas. Whip cream and sweeten; spread over fruit. Sprinkle with remaining cereal crumbs. Refrigerate.

## Cheesecake

1 1/4 cups graham cracker
   crumbs
1/4 cup melted butter or
   margarine
8 ounces cream cheese,
   softened
1/2 cup sugar
1 tablespoon lemon juice
1/2 teaspoon vanilla
1/8 teaspoon salt
2 eggs, beaten
1 cup sour cream
2 tablespoons sugar
1/2 teaspoon vanilla

Combine cracker crumbs and butter. Pat into 8-inch pie pan or 8-inch-square pan. Combine cream cheese, sugar, lemon juice, vanilla, salt and eggs. Pour into crust.

Bake at 350° for 25 to 30 minutes. Mix sour cream, sugar and vanilla. Pour over hot, baked cheese cake. Bake 10 minutes longer. Cool. Refrigerate or freeze. Can be served with fruit topping.

Serves 8.

## Strawberry Cheesecake

1 graham cracker crust,
  made according to
  package directions for
  pie pan
1 3-ounce package
  strawberry Jell-o
1 cup boiling water
1 8-ounce package cream
  cheese, softened
1 cup sugar
1 13-ounce can evaporated
  milk, chilled
1 10-ounce package frozen
  strawberries
Cool bowl and beaters

Pat graham cracker crust into 9-by-13-inch pan. Dissolve Jell-o in 1 cup boiling water. Add frozen strawberries. Cool. Beat cream cheese and sugar until fluffy. In separate chilled bowl, whip evaporated milk. Fold all together. Pour over crust.

Chill in refrigerator for several hours. Garnish each piece with a fresh strawberry. Freezes well. Thaw in refrigerator before serving.

## Individual Cherry Cheesecakes

**Serve alone or with other "finger desserts."**

16 ounces cream cheese,
  softened
3/4 cup sugar
2 eggs
1 teaspoon vanilla
24 vanilla wafers
1 can cherry pie filling

Beat cheese and sugar until creamy. Add eggs and vanilla; mix well. Put a vanilla wafer in bottom of each of 24 cupcake liners. Spoon cheese mixture into each.

Bake in muffin pan at 350° for 20 minutes. Remove from tins, and cool. Top with cherry pie filling. *Chill overnight before serving.* Freezes well. Serves 24.

# Jiffy Shortcake

**An easy base for your fresh fruit shortcakes!**

1 cup self-rising flour
1 cup vanilla ice cream
   softened

Mix flour and ice cream. Drop by spoonful onto ungreased cookie sheet or cake pan.

Bake at 400° for about 15 minutes, or until light brown.

Makes 6 shortcakes.

# Mandarin Orange Cake

**Lasts up to a week, but if people are near it,
the cake will not survive!**

2 cups flour
2 eggs
2 teaspoons baking soda
2 cups sugar
2 teaspoons vanilla
1 teaspoon salt
2 11-ounce cans mandarin
   oranges

*Glaze:*
1 1/2 cups brown sugar
6 tablespoons butter
6 tablespoons milk

Remove excess liquid from oranges, but do not completely drain. Combine all ingredients. Beat until well-blended and oranges are broken up.

Bake in 9-by-13-inch greased pan at 325° for 30 to 35 minutes.

Combine all glaze ingredients in a saucepan. Boil for 3 minutes, stirring constantly. Make holes in hot cake with fork. Pour hot glaze over cake. Serve with whipped cream.

## Cranberry Bundt Cake

1 package yellow cake mix
1 small package instant
    vanilla pudding
1/2 cup vegetable oil
4 eggs
1 cup warm water
1/3 cup poppy seeds
2 cups fresh cranberries,
    rinsed

Soak poppy seeds in water for about 10 minutes. Mix all ingredients for 2 minutes with electric mixer.

Bake at 350° for 1 hour to 1 hour and 15 minutes in well-greased tube or bundt pan. Cool cake in pan for 10 minutes. Remove to rack to finish cooling.

## Apple Cake

1/4 cup margarine
1 cup sugar
1 egg
1 cup flour
1 teaspoon baking soda
1/2 teaspoon salt
3/4 teaspoon cinnamon
2 1/4 cups peeled, raw
    apples, coarsely grated
1/2 cup chopped nuts
1/2 cup raisins
2 teaspoons vanilla

Cream margarine, sugar and egg. Sift flour, soda, salt and cinnamon. Add the dry ingredients to the creamed mixture in thirds, blending well after each addition. Add the apples, nuts, raisins and vanilla. Stir until thoroughly mixed. Spread into greased 8-by-8-inch pan.

Bake at 350° for 45 minutes, or until toothpick inserted in center comes out clean.

Sift powdered sugar over cake, when it has cooled slightly. Serve with whipped topping, if desired.

Makes 9 to 12 servings.

## Chocolate Bundt Cake

**Teachers' lounge favorite.**

1 box fudge brownie mix
1 box coconut almond or
    coconut pecan frosting
    mix
1 cup sour cream
2/3 cup milk
2 eggs

Combine all ingredients in a bowl. Mix well. Pour into greased and floured bundt pan.

Bake at 350° for about 70 minutes, or until inserted toothpick comes out clean. Cool. Remove from pan. Sprinkle with powdered sugar.

## Lumberjack Chocolate Sheet Cake

**This big cake is moist and delicious.**

2 cups sugar
2 cups flour
1 teaspoon salt
1 teaspoon baking soda
1 cup butter
1 cup water
4 tablespoons cocoa
1/2 cup sour cream
2 eggs

*Frosting:*
1 cup butter
6 tablespoons condensed
    milk
2 tablespoons cocoa
1 teaspoon vanilla
1 box (scant 4 cups)
    powdered sugar, sifted

Mix sugar, flour, salt and soda. Combine the butter, water and cocoa. Bring to a boil. Add to dry mixture. Add sour cream and eggs. Pour into a greased 11-by-17-inch jelly roll pan. Bake at 375° for 15 to 18 minutes.

Combine first 4 frosting ingredients. Bring to a boil. Add powdered sugar. Beat well.

Serves 20 easily.

## Date-Chocolate Picnic Cake

**This moist cake has a "baked-in" topping, and travels very well.**

1 cup chopped dates
1 1/2 cups boiling water
1 teaspoon baking soda
1/2 cup shortening
1/2 cup sugar
1/2 cup brown sugar
2 eggs
1 3/4 cups flour
1/4 teaspoon salt
3/4 teaspoon soda
6 ounces chocolate chips
1/2 cup brown sugar
1/2 cup chopped nuts

Mix dates, water and soda, and let cool. Cream the shortening, sugars and eggs. Combine with date mixture, and stir well. Add flour, salt and soda.

Mix chocolate chips, 1/2 cup brown sugar and nuts, and sprinkle on cake mixture.

Bake in 9-by-13-inch greased pan at 350° for 30 to 40 minutes.

## Rhubarb Cake

1/2 cup shortening
1 1/2 cups sugar
1 egg, beaten
1 teaspoon vanilla
1 teaspoon baking soda
1 cup buttermilk
2 cups flour
1/2 teaspoon salt
3 - 4 cups cut-up fresh
    rhubarb

*Glaze:*
2 tablespoons butter,
    softened
3 tablespoons milk
1 cup sifted powdered sugar

In large mixing bowl, cream shortening and sugar. Add egg. Stir in vanilla.

Pour buttermilk into a 2-cup container. Add soda. Mix. Combine dry ingredients. Add alternately to sugar mixture with buttermilk. Fold in rhubarb. Mix well.

Bake in a 9-by-13-inch greased and floured pan at 350° for 45 minutes. Combine glaze ingredients, and spread on cake.

## Mississippi Mud Cake

**Given by a Southern belle, Terry, married to an Iowa farm boy and living in Minnesota.**

1 cup margarine
2 cups sugar
1/3 cup cocoa
1 1/2 cups flour
4 eggs, beaten
1 cup coconut
1 cup pecans, coarsely
    chopped
1 7-ounce jar marshmallow
    creme

*Frosting:*
6 tablespoons margarine
1 square (1 ounce)
    unsweetened chocolate
1/4 cup milk
3 cups powdered sugar
1 teaspoon vanilla

Melt margarine. Add sugar, cocoa, flour and eggs. Beat together by hand. Fold in coconut and pecans. Pour into 9-by-13-inch greased cake pan.

Bake at 350° for 40 minutes. Remove from oven, and immediately spread marshmallow creme over cake. Let cool.

Melt margarine, chocolate and milk over low heat. Add sugar and vanilla. Spread over marshmallow creme.

## Big Lake Cake

**Ingredients are easy to take along.**

2 cans blueberry pie filling
1 box white cake mix
1/4 pound (1 stick) butter,
    melted
1 3-ounce package slivered
    almonds

Put blueberry pie filling on bottom of 9-by-13-inch, buttered pan. Sprinkle dry cake mix on top. Drizzle melted butter over cake mix. Sprinkle almonds on top.

Bake at 350° for 50 minutes.

# Carrot Cake

### Tasty and moist!

2 cups sugar
2 cups flour
2 teaspoons baking soda
2 teaspoons baking powder
2 teaspoons cinnamon
1 teaspoon salt
4 eggs, beaten
1 1/2 cups vegetable oil
3 cups shredded carrots
1/2 cup chopped pecans
1 teaspoon vanilla

Combine dry ingredients. Add remaining ingredients, mixing well.

Bake in a greased 9-by-13-inch pan at 300° for 1 hour. Check for doneness.

Combine frosting ingredients. Mix well. Spread on cake.

*Frosting:*
6 ounces cream cheese, softened
1/2 stick (1/4 cup) butter or margarine, softened
1 box (1 pound) powdered sugar, sifted
2 teaspoons vanilla

# Cherry Crunch

### Easy, good, and fast to prepare for unexpected company!

3/4 cup Bisquick
1/4 cup butter or margarine, softened
1/2 cup sugar
1/2 cup chopped nuts
1/2 teaspoon cinnamon
1 21-ounce can cherry pie filling

Pour pie filling into an ungreased 9-inch-square pan. Combine other ingredients, and sprinkle over the cherries. Bake at 350° for 25 to 30 minutes.

Serves 6 to 8.

# Crazy Cherry Cake

**It's mixed in the cake pan...no need for a mixing bowl!**

1/4 cup vegetable oil
1 white cake mix
2 eggs
1/2 cup water
1 can cherry pie filling

Spread oil around 9-by-13-inch cake pan. Add cake mix, eggs and water, combining well. Add pie filling. Mix with batter just to marbleize.

*Cream Cheese Frosting*
1 3-ounce package cream
    cheese, softened
1 tablespoon milk
1 teaspoon lemon juice
Dash of salt
2 1/2 cups powdered sugar,
    sifted

Bake at 350° for about 30 minutes, or until done.

Blend all frosting ingredients, except the sugar. Gradually add sugar, beating until smooth and of spreading consistency. If too thick, stir in additional milk, 1 teaspoon at a time.

# Nötkaka

**A nutcake recipe from Sweden, where they use hazel nuts. Our own pecans or walnuts will do.**

3 eggs
1 cup sugar
1 6-ounce package
    chopped nuts
1/2 teaspoon baking powder

Beat eggs and sugar. Add nuts and baking powder.

Bake in well-greased and sugared 8-by-8-inch pan at 350° for 40 minutes. Serve with whipped cream.

Serves 9.

## Choc-Dot Pumpkin Cake or Cupcakes

2 cups sifted all-purpose
    flour
2 teaspoons baking powder
1 teaspoon baking soda
1/2 teaspoon salt
1 1/2 teaspoons cinnamon
1/2 teaspoon ground cloves
1/4 teaspoon allspice
1/4 teaspoon ginger
2 cups sugar
4 eggs
1 16-ounce can pumpkin
1 cup vegetable oil
1 cup All Bran cereal
1 6-ounce package chocolate
    chips
1 cup chopped nuts

*Lemon glaze:*
2 tablespoons butter
1 1/2 cups confectioner's
    sugar
2 teaspoons lemon juice
2 tablespoons orange juice

Sift flour, baking powder, soda, salt, spices and sugar. Set aside. In a large bowl, beat eggs until foamy. Add pumpkin, oil and bran. Mix well. Add sifted dry ingredients, mixing only until combined. Stir in chocolate chips and nuts. Fill miniature greased cupcake pans 2/3 full.

Bake at 350° for 15 to 28 minutes. Cool.

Cream all glaze ingredients. Glaze cupcakes. You may also bake this recipe in a tube pan for about 70 minutes. Cool completely before removing from pan. Freezes well.

Makes about 100 small cupcakes.

## Minnesota Sundae

**The sweet and salty topping is a good combination!**

Top vanilla ice cream with honey and sunflower seeds.

# Berry Pie

**This pie is especially good with wild blueberries. Note that this crust does not require a rolling pin!**

*Crust:*
**2 cups flour**
**1 1/4 teaspoons salt**
**2 teaspoons sugar**
**2/3 cup salad oil**
**3 tablespoons milk**

*Filling:*
**4 cups berries**
**1 cup sugar**
**1/4 cup flour**
**1/4 teaspoon cinnamon**
**1/8 teaspoon nutmeg**
**1/8 teaspoon cloves**
**2 tablespoons margarine**
**    or butter**

Mix flour, salt, sugar, oil and milk together in 8-by-8-inch pan. Reserve 1 cup of the mixture to sprinkle on top. Pat rest in bottom of pan.

Mix berries and dry ingredients. Put over crust. Dot with margarine. Sprinkle reserved crust mixture on top. Bake at 400° for 40 to 50 minutes.

# Easy Refrigerator Pie

**This recipe makes two pies. No baking necessary!**

**2 prepared graham cracker**
**    crusts**
**1 6-ounce can frozen**
**    lemonade, thawed**
**1 14-ounce can sweetened**
**    condensed milk**
**1 8-ounce container**
**    Cool Whip**
**1 14-ounce can crushed**
**    pineapple, drained**
**Yellow food coloring, a few**
**    drops (optional)**

Combine lemonade and milk. Add other ingredients, and mix well. Divide mixture between two pie shells. Chill at least two hours before eating. May be frozen. Delicious as is, or may top with a blueberry sauce.

These two pies will serve 12.

## Chocolate Amaretto Pie

**Our neighbors serve this for special guests at their cabin on Lower Cullen Lake.**

1 1/2 cups chocolate Oreo
  cookie crumbs
1/4 cup soft butter
1 tablespoon sugar
1 quart chocolate ice cream
1/3 cup Amaretto liqueur
1 cup heavy cream
2 tablespoons Amaretto
Chocolate sprinkles

Mix crumbs, butter and sugar. Press mixture into ungreased 9-inch pie pan. Chill. Soften ice cream. Stir in 1/3 cup Amaretto. Pour into chilled pie shell. Mix cream and 2 tablespoons Amaretto. Beat until stiff. Pile whipped cream in mounds around edge of pie. Freeze. Take out 10 minutes before serving.

Serves 6 to 8.

## Apple Crisp

Apples, peeled and sliced
Cinnamon
1 teaspoon salt
1/4 cup water
1 cup flour
1 1/4 cups sugar
1/2 cup butter

In a 9-by-13-inch buttered pan, put enough apples to fill 3/4 full. Sprinkle with cinnamon to taste, salt and water. Combine the flour, sugar and butter. Sprinkle over the apples.

Bake at 350° for 40 minutes. Serve warm with cream or ice cream.

Serves 6.

# No Crust Pumpkin Pie

### Serve warm with ice cream. Try butter brickle!

4 eggs
3/4 cup sugar
1 teaspoon ginger
1 teaspoon cinnamon
1/2 teaspoon salt
1 16-ounce can pumpkin
1 cup milk

Beat eggs. Add sugar and spices. Mix in salt and pumpkin. Blend in milk, and stir until mixture is smooth. Pour into greased 9-inch pie pan.

Bake at 325° for 50 minutes, until firm or when knife inserted in filling 2 inches from center comes out clean.

# Apple Pie Pudding

### This tastes good whether warm or cold.

2 large tart cooking apples,
    peeled and thinly sliced
3/4 cup brown sugar
1/2 cup self-rising flour
1/4 cup butter
1/2 cup chopped pecans

Arrange apples in layers in loaf pan or baking dish. Sprinkle each layer with brown sugar, using about 1/2 cup. Mix together remaining sugar and flour. Cream in the butter. Add pecans. Put this on top of apples.

Bake at 350° for 45 minutes. You may wish to serve this with poured cream.

Serves 4.

## Brown Rice Pudding

**White rice may be used instead of brown.**

2 cups cooked brown rice
(a scant 3/4 cup,
uncooked)
3 cups milk
3 eggs, beaten
3/4 cup brown sugar or
honey
1 cup raisins
Sprinklings of nutmeg
and/or cinnamon
(optional)

Mix all ingredients. Spread in a buttered casserole or 9-by-13-inch pan.

Bake at 350° for 1 hour. Serve in sauce dishes—pass the cream to pour over it. Good warm or cold!

Serves 10 to 12.

## Frozen Chocolate Cream Pie

1  4-ounce package Baker's
German sweet chocolate
1/3 cup milk
2 tablespoons sugar
1  3-ounce package cream
cheese, softened
3 1/2 cups (1 8-ounce container) Cool Whip,
thawed
8-inch graham cracker crust

Heat chocolate and 2 table-spoons of the milk in sauce-pan over low heat, stirring until chocolate is melted. Beat sugar into cream cheese. Add remaining milk and the chocolate mixture. Beat until smooth. Fold in Cool Whip, blending until smooth. Spoon into crust.

Freeze until firm, about 4 hours. Garnish with chocolate curls, if desired. Remove from freezer 10 minutes before serving. Store any left-over pie in the freezer.

# Favorite Refrigerator Dessert

## A good choice when feeding a crowd.

1 cup flour
1/2 cup nuts
1/2 cup margarine
1 8-ounce package cream
    cheese
1 cup powdered sugar
1 large container Cool Whip
2 packages instant pudding,
    any flavor
3 cups milk
Nuts, chopped (optional)

Mix together flour and nuts. Cut in margarine, as for pie crust. Press into ungreased 9-by-13-inch pan. Bake at 350° for 15 minutes. Cool.

Cream together cream cheese and powdered sugar. Add 1 cup Cool Whip to creamed mixture. Spread over cooled crust.

Beat together instant pudding and milk. Spread over cream cheese layer. Spread remaining Cool Whip over pudding layer. Sprinkle with nuts. Refrigerate for several hours or overnight.

Serves 20.

# Creme de Coffee Dessert

### Simple...and the men love it!

**Coffee-flavored ice cream**
**Creme de Cacao (liqueur or flavoring)**
**Pecans or almonds, well-toasted**

Toast nuts in advance by baking in a shallow pan at 350° for 10 to 20 minutes. For each serving of ice cream, top with 2 tablespoons of Creme de Cacao. Sprinkle with nuts.

# Quick Summer Trifle

**1 white Jiffy cake mix (8 1/2 ounces)**
**Fresh fruit—peaches, strawberries, blueberries, etc.**
**1 package French vanilla instant pudding**
**3-ounce package cream cheese, softened**
**8-ounce carton Cool Whip, or 1 cup whipping cream, whipped and sweetened**

Prepare cake mix according to directions. Bake at 350° in a *9-by-13-inch* pan. Test for doneness after 15 minutes. When cooled, cover cake with a layer of sliced fresh fruit.

Prepare pudding according to directions, and mix with cream cheese. Spread over fruit. Cover with Cool Whip. Refrigerate.

Serves 12 to 15.

# Schaum Torte

### This will melt in your mouth.

*Meringue Crust:*
**4 egg whites**
**1/4 teaspoon cream of tartar**
**1 cup sugar**

*Filling:*
**4 egg yolks, well-beaten**
**1/2 cup sugar**
**3 tablespoons lemon juice**
**Lemon rind, grated, from
    one lemon**
**1 cup whipping cream**
**1 tablespoon powdered
    sugar**

Beat egg whites until frothy. Add cream of tartar, and beat. Gradually add sugar, beating until stiff and glossy. Spread in a well-greased pie pan. Bake for 1 hour: 275 ° for first 20 minutes; 300 ° for next 40 minutes.

Cook egg yolks, sugar, lemon juice and rind, stirring constantly, until thick. When crust and filling are cool, whip the cream, sweetening it with powdered sugar. Spread 1/2 of the whipped cream on the crust, then the lemon filling, and top with remaining whipped cream. Refrigerate. Can make 12 to 24 hours in advance.

Serves 6, or 8 if necessary.

# Cookies & Bars

## Tried-and-True Sugar Cookies

1 cup margarine, softened
1 cup powdered sugar
1 cup sugar
1 cup (scant) vegetable oil
2 eggs, well-beaten
1 teaspoon vanilla
4 cups all-purpose flour
1/2 teaspoon salt
1 teaspoon baking soda
1 teaspoon cream of tartar

Cream margarine and sugars. Add oil, eggs and vanilla. Mix. Mix dry ingredients, and stir into sugar mixture. Chill at least two hours.

Place 1-inch balls on ungreased cookie sheet. Flatten with glass dipped in sugar.

Bake at 350° for 12 to 15 minutes.

Makes about 100 cookies.

## Oatmeal-Coconut Cookies

1/2 cup butter or margarine
1/2 cup shortening
1 cup sugar
1 cup brown sugar
2 eggs, beaten
1 teaspoon vanilla
1 cup flour
1 1/2 teaspoons baking
    powder
1 teaspoon baking soda
1/2 teaspoon salt
2 cups dry oatmeal
2 cups coconut (can substi-
    tute chocolate chips or
    raisins)

Cream butter, shortening and sugars. Add eggs and vanilla. Sift flour, baking powder, soda and salt. Add to first mixture. Add oatmeal and coconut. Form dough into balls.

Bake at 350° until brown, about 12 minutes.

## Peanut Butter Cookies

**Excellent for anyone allergic to wheat—and for
peanut butter lovers!**

1 cup peanut butter
1 cup sugar
1 teaspoon baking powder
1 egg, beaten

Mix ingredients well. Roll into balls the size of walnuts.

Bake at 325° for about 10
minutes.

Makes about 3 dozen
cookies.

## Grandma's Ginger Cookies

1/4 cup butter
1/2 cup Crisco
1 cup sugar
1 egg
1 teaspoon cinnamon
1 teaspoon cloves
1 teaspoon ginger
4 tablespoons molasses
2 teaspoons baking soda
2 1/4 cups flour

Cream shortenings and sugar.
Add remaining ingredients.
Mix together. Chill dough.
Roll into size of large marble.
Dip into sugar.

Bake at 350° for 10 minutes.
If you want cracks on the
top, sprinkle a few drops of
water on each cookie before
baking.

# Unbaked Cookies

2 cups carob chips or
    chocolate chips
1 cup peanut butter
1 6-ounce bag chow mein
    noodles
Spanish peanuts or sun-
    flower seeds

Melt chips. Stir in peanut butter, until well-blended. Add chow mein noodles and nuts or seeds. Drop by tea-spoonful onto waxed paper. Let set to harden.

# Moravian Sugar Cookies

### A great sheet cookie. Cut after baking.

1/2 cup butter, softened
1 cup sugar
1 teaspoon baking powder
1 teaspoon vanilla
1/4 teaspoon salt
1 egg
1 1/4 cups flour

Combine butter, sugar, baking powder, vanilla and salt. Blend in egg and flour. Spread out half of dough on a well-greased cookie sheet. It will make a rectangle about 8-by-10 inches.

*Topping:*
1/4 cup sugar
2 teaspoons cinnamon
1/4 cup finely chopped nuts
    (optional)

Combine topping ingredients and spread half of it over the dough.

Bake at 350° for 12 to 15 minutes, or until golden brown on edges. Cool 1 minute. Cut into squares or rectangles, and remove from pan while warm.

Repeat the process with remaining half of dough and topping.

## Toasted Coconut Cookies

**Delightfully delicious and easy to make.**

2  3 3/8-ounce packages
   instant toasted coconut
   pudding
1 1/2 cups margarine
2 1/2 cups flour

Mix all ingredients. Shape into balls and flatten.

Bake at 350° for 15 minutes.

Makes 6 dozen cookies.


## Soda Cracker Cookies

**Very good!**

35 soda crackers
1 cup brown sugar
1 cup butter
12 ounces chocolate chips
1/2 cup chopped walnuts

Line a 10-by-15-inch pan with
foil. Place crackers on the
foil. Boil the brown sugar
and butter for 3 minutes.
Spread over the crackers.

Bake at 400° for 5 minutes.
In the meantime, melt chocolate chips. When crackers
have been removed from
oven and the bubbling has
stopped (about 1 minute),
spread melted chocolate on
top. Sprinkle with nuts. Pan
may be put in freezer for
faster cooling. Cut or break
into serving-sized pieces.

Makes about 35 pieces.

# Monster Cookies

**Right out of Paul Bunyan's kitchen. Get out
your biggest mixing bowl!**

4 cups sugar
2 cups (1 pound) margarine
2 pounds (4 1/2 cups)
   brown sugar
3 pounds crunchy peanut
   butter
1 dozen eggs
1 tablespoon vanilla
8 teaspoons baking soda
18 cups oatmeal (a 2-pound,
   10-ounce box)
1 pound M&M's candies
1 pound chocolate chips

Combine first 7 ingredients. Mix very well. Add last 3 ingredients. Mix well. Make each cookie from dough about the size of a golf ball, then flatten out by hand.

Bake at 350° for 10 to 15 minutes, depending on size of cookie.

Note: The source of this recipe is a mother who makes the dough at home, takes it to the cabin, and bakes a few dozen cookies at a time. They are large and filling. The dough keeps well in the refrigerator for quite awhile. On your first try, you might want to make half the recipe.

## No-Bake Peanut Butter Drops

1 cup sugar
1/4 cup margarine
1/4 cup milk
1 1/2 cups quick-cooking
    oatmeal
2 1/2 tablespoons creamy
    peanut butter
1/4 cup chopped nuts
1/2 teaspoon vanilla

Combine sugar, margarine and milk in saucepan. Boil for 1 minute. Pour, while hot, over oatmeal and peanut butter. Add nuts and vanilla. Mix. Drop by teaspoonful onto wax paper. Let stand until firm.

## Snickerdoodles

1 cup soft shortening
1 1/2 cups sugar
2 eggs, beaten
2 3/4 cups flour
2 teaspoons cream of tartar
1 teaspoon baking soda
1/2 teaspoon salt
3 tablespoons sugar
3 teaspoons cinnamon

Mix shortening, 1 1/2 cups sugar and eggs. Sift flour, cream of tartar, soda and salt. Add to first mixture. Chill.

Mix 3 tablespoons sugar and cinnamon. Roll dough into balls the size of a small walnut. Roll in sugar-cinnamon mixture. Place about 2 inches apart on ungreased cookie sheet.

Bake at 400° for 8 to 10 minutes. Cookies should be lightly browned, but still soft.

Makes about 5 dozen.

# Nut Goody Bars

**You don't need an oven for these unbaked goodies.**

1 12-ounce package
   chocolate chips
1 12-ounce package
   butterscotch chips
1 cup peanut butter
1 10 1/2-ounce package
   miniature marshmallows
1 12-ounce can cocktail
   peanuts

Combine and melt first 3 ingredients. Cool slightly. Add marshmallows and peanuts. Spread in a 9-by-13-inch pan. Cool. Cut.

# Sour Cream Raisin Bars

**Travels well.**

2 cups raisins
1 cup brown sugar
1 cup butter
1 1/3 cups quick-cooking
   oatmeal
1 teaspoon baking soda
1 3/4 cups flour
3 egg yolks
1 1/2 cups sour cream
1 cup sugar
2 1/2 tablespoons cornstarch
1 teaspoon vanilla

Cook raisins in small amount of water for 10 minutes. Drain, and cool. Cream brown sugar and butter. Add oatmeal, soda and flour. Put half the mixture in a 9-by-13-inch pan.

Bake at 350° for 7 minutes. In a saucepan, mix egg yolks, sour cream, sugar and cornstarch. Simmer, stirring constantly. Add raisins and vanilla. Pour over baked crust. Crumble remaining oatmeal mixture over top. Bake 30 minutes more.

# Mixed Nut Bars

### These are delicious!

1 1/2 cups flour
1/2 cup butter
3/4 cup brown sugar
Dash of salt
2 cups mixed nuts
1/2 cup light corn syrup
1 cup butterscotch chips
2 tablespoons butter

Mix and pat flour, butter, brown sugar and salt into ungreased 9-by-13-inch pan.

Bake for 10 minutes at 350°. Sprinkle nuts over crust. Melt syrup, chips and butter. Pour over nuts.

Bake for 10 minutes more. Cut. Chill. Store in refrigerator.

# Mounds-Type Bars

### Chocolate chips, in any form, are a family favorite.

2 cups crushed graham
    crackers
1/3 cup sugar
1/2 cup melted butter
1 package flaked coconut
1 can sweetened condensed
    milk
1 12-ounce bag chocolate
    chips

Mix the crackers, sugar and butter. Press into a 9-by-13-inch buttered pan. Sprinkle coconut over crust. Pour milk over coconut.

Bake at 350° for 15 to 20 minutes (top should be slightly brown). Melt the chocolate chips over low heat. Spread on warm bars.

## Lemon Bars

2 cups flour
1 cup butter or margarine
1 1/2 cups powdered sugar
4 eggs, slightly beaten
2 cups sugar
4 tablespoons flour
1 teaspoon baking powder
6 tablespoons lemon juice

Heat oven to 350°. Mix the flour, butter and sugar until crumbly. Pat mixture into a 9-by-13-inch pan.

Bake for 20 minutes. Mix the remaining ingredients. Pour over the cooled baked crust.

Bake for 30 minutes more. Cool. Sprinkle with powdered sugar.

Makes 24 bars.

## Lazy Day Bars

1/2 cup margarine or butter
1 1/2 cups graham cracker
    crumbs
1 14-ounce can sweetened
    condensed milk
1 6-ounce package chocolate
    chips
1  3 1/2-ounce can (1 1/3
    cups) flaked coconut
1 cup chopped nuts

In a 9-by-13-inch baking pan, melt margarine in oven. Sprinkle crumbs over margarine. Pour sweetened condensed milk evenly over crumbs. Top evenly with remaining ingredients; press down gently.

Bake at 350° (325° for a glass pan) for 25 to 30 minutes or until lightly browned. Cool thoroughly before cutting. Store, loosely covered, at room temperature.

Makes 24 bars.

## Corn Flake Bars

### Keeps well in the refrigerator.

4 cups Corn Flakes
1 cup coconut
1/3 cup slivered almonds
8 ounces marshmallows
1/3 cup margarine
1 8-ounce milk chocolate
    candy bar

Combine Corn Flakes, coconut and almonds in a 9-by-13-inch pan. Warm in a 250° oven. Melt marshmallows and margarine. Combine Corn Flake mixture with marshmallow mixture.

Pat into 9-by-13-inch pan. Melt the chocolate bar. Spread over top. Cut into squares.

## Carrot Bars

1 15-ounce jar (1 2/3 cups)
    applesauce
3 eggs
1/3 cup vegetable oil
1 box Carrot 'n Spice
    cake mix
1 cup raisins

*Topping:*
1 can cream cheese frosting
1/2 cup chopped nuts
    (optional)

In large bowl, blend applesauce, eggs and oil. Mix for 1 minute at low speed. Add cake mix. Blend until moistened, then beat for 2 minutes at medium speed. Stir in raisins. Spread in greased and floured 10-by-15-inch pan or in two 8- or 9-inch-square pans.

Bake at 350° for 25 to 35 minutes, or until toothpick comes out clean. Cool.

Spread frosting over bars. Sprinkle with nuts. These bars are best if refrigerated.

# Angel Food Bars

## Soooo easy and soooo good!

1 box angel food cake mix
    (1-step type)
1 can lemon pie filling
1 cup flaked coconut

*Glaze:*
2 cups powdered sugar,
    sifted
Juice from small lemon
Milk

Combine dry cake mix and pie filling. Beat for about 5 minutes. Add coconut. Mix well. Pour into jelly roll pan or 9-by-13-inch pan, which has been greased and floured.

Bake at 350° for 20 to 25 minutes.

Mix powdered sugar and lemon juice. Add enough milk (a teaspoon at a time) to make a rather thin glaze. When bars are cool, spread the glaze on top.

# Graham Cracker Bars

Graham crackers
1 cup brown sugar
1 cup butter
1/2 - 1 cup chopped nuts
    (walnuts, pecans or
    sliced almonds)
1 cup milk chocolate chips
    (optional)

Line brownie pan (10-by-15-inch) with foil. Cover with graham crackers. Combine brown sugar and butter. Boil for 2 minutes. Pour over crackers. Sprinkle with nuts and chocolate chips.

Bake at 350° for 5 minutes. Remove each cracker from pan, and place on wax paper.

## Cream Cheese Bars

1 stick (1/2 cup) butter or
  margarine
1 box yellow cake mix
  (without pudding
  added)
1 egg
1 box powdered sugar
1 teaspoon vanilla
1 8-ounce package cream
  cheese, softened
2 eggs

Preheat oven to 300°. Melt butter in 9-by-13-inch pan in the preheating oven. Pour melted butter into mixing bowl, leaving cake pan "greased." Combine cake mix, egg and melted butter. Mix well. Pat into cake pan. On low speed, mix the powdered sugar, vanilla, cream cheese and 2 eggs. Pour over base.

Bake for 45 to 50 minutes, until top is golden brown.

## Pumpkin Bars

2 cups flour
2 teaspoons baking powder
1 teaspoon baking soda
1/2 teaspoon salt
2 teaspoons cinnamon
2 cups sugar
4 eggs
1 cup vegetable oil
1 15-ounce can pumpkin

*Cream Cheese Frosting:*
3 ounces cream cheese,
  softened
6 tablespoons butter
1 teaspoon milk
1 teaspoon vanilla
1 3/4 cup powdered sugar

Sift together dry ingredients. Add beaten eggs, pumpkin and oil.

Bake in jelly roll pan at 350° for 25 minutes.

Blend all frosting ingredients. Spread on cake.

# Salty Nut Bars

**The saltiness and sweetness is a great combination!**

1 1/2 cups flour
3/4 cup brown sugar
1/2 teaspoon salt
1/2 cup butter or margarine
1 12-ounce can mixed salted
    nuts or peanuts

*Butterscotch Topping:*
1 12-ounce package
    butterscotch chips
1/2 cup light corn syrup
2 tablespoons butter
1 teaspoon vanilla

Mix first 4 ingredients with a pastry blender. Pat into 9-by-13-inch buttered, or non-stick, pan.

Bake for 10 minutes at 350°. Sprinkle nuts over baked layer.

Melt butterscotch topping ingredients over low heat, stirring constantly. Spread over nuts.

Bake for 10 minutes at 350°. Cut into squares while still a little warm.

# Candy Bar Bars

4 cups oatmeal
1 cup brown sugar
2/3 cup butter
1/2 cup light corn syrup
2 teaspoons vanilla
1 cup (6 ounces) chocolate
    chips
2/3 cup peanut butter

Mix oatmeal and brown sugar. Melt butter and corn syrup. Add vanilla. Combine two mixtures. Pat into 9-by-13-inch pan.

Bake at 375° for 10 to 12 minutes. Cool. Melt chips and peanut butter. Spread on bars.

## Speedy Little Devils

1 Duncan Hines Deluxe II
  Devils Food cake mix
1/2 cup margarine or butter,
  melted
3/4 cup creamy peanut
  butter
1 7- or 7 1/2-ounce jar
  marshmallow creme

Combine melted butter and dry cake mix. Reserve 1 1/2 cups of this mixture for top crust. Pat remaining mixture into ungreased 9-by-13-inch pan. Top with combined peanut butter and marshmallow creme, and spread evenly over first layer. Crumble remaining mixture over that.

Bake for 20 minutes at 350°. Cool.

Makes 3 dozen bars.

## Chocolate Scotcheroos

1 cup sugar
1 cup light corn syrup
1 cup peanut butter
6 cups Rice Krispies
1 6-ounce package chocolate
  chips
1 6-ounce package butter-
  scotch chips

Combine sugar and syrup in a 3-quart saucepan. Cook over low heat, stirring constantly, just until mixture boils. Remove from heat. Blend in peanut butter. Stir in Rice Krispies. Press into buttered 9-by-13-inch pan. Melt the chips over hot water. Spread on top. Cut into 30 bars.

# Marble Squares

**A favorite of our daughters for pot luck at the cabin.
Stays moist.**

8 ounces cream cheese
1/3 cup sugar
1 egg
1/2 cup margarine
3/4 cup water
1 1/2  1-ounce squares
    unsweetened chocolate
2 cups flour
2 cups sugar
2 eggs
1/2 cup (4 ounces)
    sour cream
1 cup (6 ounces)
    chocolate chips
1 teaspoon baking soda
1/2 teaspoon salt

Combine softened cream cheese and sugar, mixing until well-blended. Add egg. Mix well. Combine margarine, water and chocolate squares in saucepan. Bring to a boil. Remove from heat. Stir in combined flour and sugar. Add eggs, sour cream, baking soda and salt. Mix well.

Pour into greased and floured 15 1/2-by-10 1/2-inch jelly roll pan. Spoon cheese mixture over chocolate batter. Cut through batter with a knife several times for marble effect. Sprinkle with chocolate chips.

Bake at 375° for 25 to 30 minutes. Cut into squares.

## Caramel Layer Chocolate Squares

**Travels beautifully, if there are any left when you leave home.**

1 package Kraft caramels
1 5.3-ounce can evaporated
    milk
1 German chocolate cake
    mix
3/4 cup butter or margarine,
    melted
1 cup chopped nuts
1 cup chocolate chips

In saucepan, combine caramels and 1/3 cup milk (half of the can). Cook over low heat, stirring until melted. Set aside. Grease and flour 9-by-13-inch pan. In large bowl, combine cake mix, butter, 1/3 cup milk and nuts. By hand, stir the dough until it holds together. Press 1/2 of dough into pan.

Bake at 350° for 6 minutes. Remove from oven. Sprinkle with chocolate chips. Spread caramel mixture over chips. Spread rest of dough over caramels.

Bake 15 to 18 minutes. Cool in refrigerator for 30 minutes, or overnight.

# Caramel Krispies

**Unwrap the caramels while sitting on the dock.**

**1 14-ounce bag Kraft
    caramels
3 tablespoons water
5 cups Rice Krispies
1 cup peanuts
1 cup chocolate chips
1 cup butterscotch chips**

Melt caramels with water in saucepan over low heat. Stir frequently, until sauce is smooth. Pour over cereal and nuts. Toss until well-coated. With greased fingers, press mixture into a greased 9-by-13-inch pan. Sprinkle chips on top.

Place in 200° oven for 5 minutes or until chips soften. Spread chips until blended to form frosting. Cool for at least 10 minutes. Cut into bars.

## Walnut Shortbread Squares

1 pound (2 cups) butter,
    softened
1 cup sugar
1 cup walnut pieces,
    coarsely ground
2 teaspoons vanilla
1/4 teaspoon salt
4 cups flour, sifted

Cream butter and sugar until light and fluffy. Beat the walnuts, vanilla and salt into the creamed mixture. Add the flour. Mix well. Spoon the dough into a lightly greased jelly roll pan (10-by-15 1/2-inch) and smooth it out, as dough will not change shape as it bakes.

Bake at 325° for about 45 minutes, or until lightly browned. Cool in pan. Cut into bars. Store in covered container. Keeps well for weeks.

Makes about 75 1-by-2-inch bars.

# No-Bake Brownies

### No oven? No problem!

1 cup chopped walnuts
4 cups graham cracker crumbs
1/2 cup sifted powdered sugar
2 tablespoons dry instant coffee
12 ounces semi-sweet chocolate chips
1 cup evaporated milk
1 teaspoon vanilla

Combine walnuts, crumbs and sugar in large bowl. Heat the coffee, chocolate chips and milk over low heat. Stir constantly until smoothly blended. Remove from heat. Add vanilla. Reserve 1/2 cup of chocolate mixture. Mix remaining chocolate with crumb mixture. Spread evenly in well-buttered 9-by-9-inch pan. Spread reserved chocolate mixture over top for glaze.

Chill until ready to serve. Keep refrigerated.

Makes 32 bars.

# Blond Brownies

1/3 cup butter
1 cup brown sugar
2 eggs
1 teaspoon vanilla
1/2 cup walnuts
1/2 cup chocolate chips
1 cup sifted flour
1/2 teaspoon baking powder
1/8 teaspoon baking soda
1/2 teaspoon salt

Cream butter and sugar. Add remaining ingredients. Mix. Pour into a greased and floured 9-by-9-inch pan.

Bake at 350° for 20 to 25 minutes. For a double recipe, use a 9-by-13-inch pan, and bake for 30 minutes.

Makes 18 bars.

# Cream Cheese Brownies

**These delicious brownies have a mix as the base.**

*Brown layer:*
1 chocolate brownie mix
1/4 cup vegetable oil
2 or 3 eggs (depending
    upon box directions)
1 teaspoon almond extract

*White layer:*
8 ounces cream cheese
4 tablespoons butter
1 1/2 cups sugar
2 eggs
2 tablespoons flour
1 teaspoon vanilla

Follow directions on box for cake-like brownies, adding 1 teaspoon almond extract. Spread in 9-by-13-inch pan.

Cream butter and cream cheese. Blend in all other white layer ingredients. Zig-zag cream cheese mixture through the brownie mixture, using a knife or fork.

Bake at 350° for 35 minutes.

# Hershey's Chocolate Brownies

## A moist brownie for chocolate lovers.

1/2 cup (1 stick) butter or
    margarine
1 cup sugar
1 can (1 pound) Hershey's
    syrup
1 cup flour
4 eggs
1/2 teaspoon salt
1 teaspoon vanilla
3/4 cup chopped nuts

*Frosting:*
1 cup sugar
4 tablespoons (1/2 stick)
    butter
1/4 cup milk
1/2 cup chocolate chips

Cream shortening and sugar.
Add remaining ingredients.
Mix well—for about 4
minutes. Spread on an 11-by-
16-inch jelly roll pan.

Bake at 350° for 20 minutes,
or until done.

Boil sugar, butter and milk
for 1 minute. Remove from
heat. Add chocolate chips.
Stir until smooth. Immediately spread on brownies.

# Kay's Chocolate Fudge

2 cups sugar
1  5.3-ounce can evaporated
    milk
10 regular-sized marsh-
    mallows
1  6-ounce package chocolate
    chips
1/4 pound (1 stick) butter,
    cut up
1 teaspoon vanilla

Combine sugar, milk and
marshmallows in a heavy
pan. Bring to a boil, stirring
constantly. Pour over chocolate chips, butter and vanilla,
mixing well. Pour into 9-by-
9-inch pan. Cool. Refrigerate.

## Chocolate Candies

**Enjoy directly from the freezer!**

**2 squares unsweetened
   baking chocolate
1 can sweetened condensed
   milk
Dash of salt
1 teaspoon vanilla
Crushed nutmeats and/or
   flaked coconut**

Mix chocolate, milk and salt together. Stir over low heat until thick. Add vanilla, and let cool somewhat, stirring occasionally.

Before it cools completely, roll into small balls, and roll in nutmeats or coconut. Refrigerate.

## S'mores

**Fun around the fireplace or campfire. The name S'mores
comes from "you want some more?"**

**Graham crackers
Marshmallows
Milk chocolate candy bars**

Place a cracker-sized piece of chocolate on graham cracker. Toast a marshmallow over the coals in the fireplace or the campfire. Put toasted marshmallow on chocolate. Top with second graham cracker.

# Beverages

# Fruit Crush

**The base for this refreshing summer drink may be stored in your freezer until needed. Great to have on hand when you're expecting company.**

3 cups water
2 cups sugar
1 46-ounce can pineapple
   juice
1 1/2 cups orange juice
1/4 cup lemon juice
3 ripe bananas, mashed
3 quarts ginger ale or
   sparkling water, chilled

In a large kettle, mix water and sugar. Bring to a boil. Remove from heat. Stir in fruit juices and mashed bananas. (Bananas can be mashed in a blender or a food processor, with a small amount of juice.) Pour into 4 ice cube freezer trays. Freeze until firm. When frozen, they can be put into plastic bags for easy cooler storage or transport.

To serve, take from freezer about 15 minutes before putting into glasses. Break up mixture, and fill glasses 1/3 full of fruit crush. Fill remainder of glass with ginger ale or sparkling water. Stir.

Makes 6 quarts, or 24 servings.

## Cranberry Punch

1 quart cranberry juice
    cocktail, chilled
2 cups pineapple juice,
    chilled
1 1/2 cups sugar
2 quarts ginger ale, chilled

Combine juices with sugar.
Just before serving, add ice
cubes and ginger ale.

Makes 28 half-cup servings.

## Mock Champagne

**Easy to make for any number of people.**

Apple cider or juice
Pineapple juice
Ginger ale

Combine equal parts of each
ingredient. Serve over ice.
The ginger ale should be a
last-minute addition.

## Cranberry Slush

**A cooling red punch.**

1 quart Ocean Spray
    cranberry juice cocktail
1 12-ounce can frozen
    lemonade
12 ounces (1 1/2 cups)
    bourbon

Mix all ingredients in a
1-gallon container, such as an
ice cream pail. Freeze.
Remove from freezer when
ready to use.

## Kool-Aid Punch for the Lake Crowd

1 large package cherry
    Kool-Aid
1 large package strawberry
    Kool-Aid
3 quarts water
2 cups sugar
1 6-ounce can frozen
    orange juice
1 6-ounce can frozen
    lemonade
1 quart ginger ale

Mix all ingredients, except
ginger ale, which should be
added just before serving.

Makes 48 half-cup servings.

## Orange Julia

1 6-ounce can frozen
    orange juice
1 cup milk
1 cup water
1/4 - 1/2 cup sugar
1 teaspoon vanilla
10 ice cubes

Mix all ingredients in blender
at low speed, gradually
adding ice cubes. Blend until
smooth.

## Easiest Lemonade

Juice of 1 large lemon
1/2 cup sugar
1 quart water

Mix. Chill. Serve over ice
cubes.

## Wine Cooler

**A good refresher for a summer day.**

Red wine
Seven-Up
Ice cubes

Choose your favorite red wine—Rose, Pink Chablis, Burgundy or Cold Duck. Place ice cubes in a tall glass. Fill 1/2 with wine and 1/2 with Seven-Up.

## Root Beer Float

For a cool treat on a hot day, remember the root beer float. Put vanilla ice cream in a tall glass, fill with root beer, and enjoy!

## Ginger Tea

**A refreshing, cool drink.**

3 tea bags
1 cup boiling water
Juice of 2 oranges
Juice of 2 lemons
1/2 cup sugar
1 28-ounce bottle ginger ale, chilled

Make a cup of strong tea by putting 3 tea bags into 1 cup boiling water. Remove bags. Add fruit juices and sugar. Chill. Just before serving, add ginger ale.

Makes about 5 8-ounce servings.

# Friendship Tea Mix

**Although usually a hot drink, try mixing this with cold water during warm weather.**

1 cup instant tea
1 14-ounce jar powdered
    orange breakfast drink
2 3-ounce packages
    lemonade mix
1 1/2 cups sugar
2 teaspoons ground cloves
2 teaspoons cinnamon

Combine all ingredients. Mix well. To serve, put 2 teaspoons of mix into cup. Fill with boiling water.

# Sun Tea

**This tea will not be bitter or cloudy, and will keep well for days. Experiment with different flavors of tea.**

Fill a 2-quart glass jar with cold water. Put 2 or 3 tea bags in jar, with tags hanging on outside. Screw on cover. Put out in the sun for 4 to 6 hours. Chill and serve over ice.

# Cocoa Mix

8-quart package dry milk
1-pound can Nestle's Quik
6-ounce jar non-dairy
    creamer
1 cup powdered sugar
1/4 teaspoon salt

Mix all ingredients. Store in tightly covered container (an ice cream bucket works well).

To serve, mix 1 part cocoa mix to 2 parts hot water.

## Margie's Mist

### Similar to a very famous liqueur.

10 ounces water
1 1/4 cups sugar
14 ounces vodka
6 heaping tablespoons
    Ovaltine
Drop of rum extract
1 pint whipping cream

Simmer water and sugar. Cool. Mix remaining ingredients with water and sugar mixture in a 2-quart container. Store in refrigerator. Shake well before serving.

## Hot Buttered Rum Mix

**A winter recipe to enjoy on a snowy day, by a crackling fire.**

1/4 pound (1 stick) butter,
    softened
1 pound dark brown sugar
1/4 teaspoon cinnamon
1/4 teaspoon nutmeg
1/4 teaspoon cloves
Rum

Cream butter and sugar. Add spices. Mix well. Store in covered container in refrigerator.

To serve, put 1 heaping tablespoon of mixture in a cup. Add 1 1/2 ounces dark rum. Fill with boiling water. Can be garnished with a cinnamon stick and lemon.

Makes 12 to 14 servings.

# Egg Coffee

**An old-fashioned way to make clear, non-bitter coffee.**

**Water**
**Coffee, regular or coarsely
   ground**
**1 egg, beaten or shaken up
   in a small, covered jar**
**Stove-top coffee pot
   (campers may use a
   covered kettle)**

Fill coffee pot 1/2 to 3/4 full of water. Bring to a boil. In a small bowl, place 1 scant tablespoon of dry coffee for each cup of water used. Pour enough beaten egg into the coffee to thoroughly moisten the grounds when mixed together with a fork. Stir moistened coffee into boiling water.

Have it boil up, but not over (hence the partially filled coffee pot). Turn down heat, and allow coffee to brew for several minutes. If you want a full pot of coffee, boil more water, and add to coffee pot. Pour about 1/2 cup cold water into pot to settle the grounds. Coffee may be kept warm on low heat. Store remaining egg in a jar for future use.

# Potpourri

# Best Ever Fudge Sauce

**Serve hot or cold.**

1 6-ounce package chocolate
   chips
1/2 cup butter
2 cups powdered sugar,
   sifted
1 1/3 cups evaporated milk
1 teaspoon vanilla

Melt chocolate and butter. Remove from heat. Add sugar and milk. Blend. Bring to a boil, stirring constantly. Cook and stir for about 8 minutes. Add vanilla.

Serve warm over ice cream. Store in covered container in refrigerator. Keeps forever!

# Fabulous Fudge Sauce

1 12-ounce package
   chocolate chips
1 cup miniature marsh-
   mallows
1 14-ounce can sweetened
   condensed milk
1/2 cup milk
1 teaspoon vanilla

Combine all ingredients. Heat slowly over low heat, until chips and marshmallows are melted. Stir occasionally.

Cool and refrigerate. May reheat for serving.

Tops 15 to 20 sundaes.

# Butterscotch Sauce

**Do not freeze. Keeps about 3 weeks in the refrigerator.**

1 pound dark brown sugar
1 cup sugar
1 cup Half and Half
1 stick butter
2 teaspoons vanilla

Combine all ingredients in top of double boiler. Cook slowly, until thick.

Tops about 12 sundaes.

## Cinnamon Blueberry Sauce

**Serve warm over waffles, pancakes, or French toast.**

1/2 cup sugar
4 teaspoons cornstarch
1/2 teaspoon grated lemon
  peel
1/4 teaspoon cinnamon
Dash of salt
2/3 cup water
1 10-ounce package frozen
  blueberries, thawed
1 teaspoon lemon juice

In a small bowl, combine
sugar, cornstarch, lemon
peel, cinnamon and salt. Set
aside.

In saucepan, combine the
water and 1/2 cup of the
blueberries. Bring to a boil.
Mash berries. Add sugar mixture, cook and stir, until
sauce thickens and bubbles.
Add remaining blueberries
and lemon juice. Simmer 3 to
5 minutes more.

Makes 2 cups.

## Strawberry Topping for Pancakes or French Toast

8 ounces cream cheese,
  softened
1 stick unsalted butter
1/2 - 3/4 cup powdered
  sugar
1 teaspoon vanilla
8 good-sized strawberries,
  mashed

Combine all ingredients. Mix
well. Store in refrigerator.

## Strawberry or Raspberry Jam for Freezer

**3 cups fresh berries, mashed**
**5 cups sugar**
**1 package powdered pectin**
**1 cup water**

Wash, hull and mash berries. Add sugar. Mix well. Let stand for about 15 minutes, stirring occasionally.

Dissolve pectin in water, and boil for 1 minute. Add water mixture to fruit. Stir for 2 minutes. Pour into freezer containers, cover, and let stand until jelled. Freeze.

This will also keep well in the refrigerator for 1 month. May also be used as a topping for ice cream or pound cake.

## Fresh Strawberry Topping

Clean and cut up fresh strawberries. Sprinkle lightly with sugar, until it suits your taste of sweetness. Chill for several hours or overnight.

Use as a topping for ice cream, shortcake, poundcake, angel food cake, pancakes, etc. You may choose to use it in combination with slightly sweetened whipped cream.

## Rhubarb Freezer Jam

2 cups rhubarb
1 cup sugar
1 3-ounce package wild
   strawberry Jell-o
1 8-ounce can crushed
   pineapple, plus liquid

Cook rhubarb and sugar until soft. Add Jell-o, pineapple and liquid.

Bring to a boil. Simmer for 15 minutes. Pour into sterilized jars. Freeze.

## Orange Sauce for Wild Game

**Serve over duck or goose.**

1 cup orange marmalade
1/2 cup orange juice
2 tablespoons freshly grated
   orange peel
2 tablespoons orange-
   flavored liqueur

Combine all ingredients in a small saucepan.

Heat over low heat, stirring until smooth.

## Parmesan Croutons

**A good way to use up extra bread.**

8 slices bread
1/4 cup butter or margarine,
   melted
1/4 cup grated Parmesan
   cheese

Remove crusts, and cube bread. Toss with melted butter and Parmesan cheese. Place on baking sheet.

Bake at 375° for about 10 minutes. When cool, store in airtight container.

## Barbecue Sauce

2 tablespoons margarine
3 buds of garlic
1 cup ketchup
1/4 cup water
2 tablespoons brown sugar
2 teaspoons liquid smoke
1 tablespoon Worcestershire
    sauce
1/2 teaspoon salt
1/4 teaspoon pepper

Slice garlic buds; brown in margarine and discard garlic. Add remaining ingredients. Simmer for 10 minutes.

Makes 1 1/2 cups.

## Best Barbecue Sauce

### Use extra sauce as a hostess gift!

1 medium onion, chopped
1/3 cup butter or margarine,
    melted
3/4 cup brown sugar
12 ounces mustard
2 ounces (1/4 cup) liquid
    smoke
1 tablespoon garlic powder
1 26-ounce bottle ketchup
1/2 cup (scant) Worcester-
    shire sauce
1/3 cup lemon juice
2 1/2 cups water

Saute onion in butter in large saucepan. Add brown sugar. Mix well. Add remaining ingredients. Bring to a boil, and simmer for 30 minutes, stirring occasionally.

Store in refrigerator. Keeps well for a long time. Delicious for hamburgers, ribs, chicken, brisket, steak, etc. Recipe doubles easily.

Makes 2 quarts.

# Hamburger To Go

Before heading for vacation, brown a large amount of hamburger with chopped onion and seasonings. Divide into usable portions, and freeze. It can serve as "ice" in the cooler enroute to your destination. Thaw, as needed, for chili, sloppy joes, lasagna, taco salad, stroganoff, spaghetti, taco pie, soup or casseroles.

# Bacon To Go

Fry a pound, or more, of bacon. Drain on paper toweling. Wrap in foil, and freeze. Thaw, as needed, for use with BLTs (bacon, lettuce, tomato sandwiches), poached eggs supreme, tossed salads, scrambled eggs or pancake batter. To serve hot, as with eggs, place under broiler or in hot frying pan for a few minutes.

# Index

# Contributors of Recipes

Peggy Alberg
Esther Allen
Ginny Anderson
Lois Anderson
Gail Barduson
Dorothy Boen
Betty Bordwell
Lola Brubacher
Olga Brubacher
Sara Brubacher
Faye Burke
Kay Burke
Sandy Burke
Mildred Burke
Hazel Cannon
Janet Carlson
Billie Cashman
Mary Choinere
Marge Coppins
Jo Crisman
Liz Cullen
Nancy Damerow
Bette Dedon
Terry Dee
Rosemary Dineen
Kathy Dirks
Eleanor Donaghy
Marie Edstrom
Georgiana Ehrlichmann
Lynn Empanger
Barb Engmark
Ole Enli
Miriam Erdahl
Char Erickson
Mary Ernst
Marian Ertl
Joyce Fargo
Kitty Felion
Michelle Felion
Margaret Feudner
Bonnie Fischer
Gerry Fleming
Trudy Forster
Bev Gerber
Barb Graf
Lucy Grams

Judy Grothe
Donna Gustafson
Francis Gustafson
Evy Hagen
Laurie Halter
Marian Hart
Jean Helgeson
Ruth Hopperstad
Gladys Jacobson
Howard Jacobson
Norma Jacobson
Larry Jeffery
Carol Johnson
Helen Johnson
Louise Jones
Betty Keunzli
Betty Kidder
Alice Kilby
Joe Knoblauch
Lorraine Knoblauch
LuAnne Knoblauch
Mary Knoblauch
Carolyn Krautkremer
Elaine Krenik
Carolyn Latz
Marilyn Lehman
Nola Lockwood
Helene Lohmann
Audrey Lommen
Sharon Magnuson
Ann Mark
Doris Maser
Elaine May
Ann McCormick
Michael McCuddin
Carol Mereness
Janine Merrick
Virginia Merrick
Kathy Mimnaugh
Alice Mol
Mona Nagel
Barb Nelson
Mary Nelson
Bernice Ness
Mary Niemann
Audrey Novak
Ruth Novotny

Marlene Olseth
Nancy Olseth
Clara Olson
Ginger Overbye
Ethel Payne
Bob Paul
Ruby Perkins
Kay Peterson
Lucille Petrak
Carol Pohle
June Raarup
Diane Rabe
Susie Redpath
Lea Rae Reese
Carolyn Ring
Jo Roseborough
Joan Ryberg
Lynne Segal
Anne Senn
Pat Shearer
Bobbie Shoemaker
Nikki Sindt
Betsy Skjervold
Dianne E. Smith
Mary Ellen Solberg
Judy Sotebeer
Sharon Stefan
Mary Straka
Gail Swalve
Pat Tagader
Irene Tanglen
Bev Thurn
Vi Towley
Carol Tveit
Shirley Velner
Lorraine Wagner
Dawn Wanous
Diana Waterbury
Perry Wegleitner
Sue Weinstein
Dorothy Welch
Carol Wentzlaff
Aileen Wigginton
Mary Lou Williams
Peg Wilhoit
Carol Witsoe

# About the Authors

*Mary Brubacher,* a resident of Hopkins, Minnesota, has had a long-time interest in collecting recipes and cookbooks and preparing special foods. She has also helped produce a cookbook for a women's group in Hopkins.

A wife and the mother of three daughters, Mary has been a "cabin person" at Little Hubert Lake, near Nisswa, Minnesota, for 19 years. She is a graduate of Hamline University, with a bachelor's degree in nursing, and is currently a school nurse in the Hopkins School District.

*Margie Knoblauch* is a Minnesota native who lives in the Minnetonka-Hopkins area of the Twin Cities. A wife and the mother of six children, she spends her summers at the family's log cabin, "Knobby Pines," near Park Rapids, Minnesota.

Margie is a University of Minnesota home economics graduate with a degree in institutional management, and has worked as a home economist for Northern States Power Company and as a representative of Admiral Corporation. She is a member of Home Economics in Homemaking, a group of home economics graduates, and has been involved in the marketing of a cookbook for that group.

Margie's family has been involved in several food-and-beverage establishments in Minnesota, including the Hopkins House, Breezy Point Resort, and Le Bistro, Inc.

# North Country
# CABIN
# COOKING

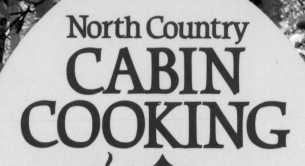

## by Mary Brubacher
## and Margie Knoblauch

More than 300 quick 'n' easy, sure-to-please
recipes chosen especially for your cabin
kitchen. Enticing appetizers and salads, hearty
soups and sandwiches, scrumptious main
dishes of every description, irresistible snacks
and desserts — all of this and more to
help you make the most of your northwoods
weekend and vacation meals.

Cover photograph by Robert Sheppard

**Garlic Press**
ISBN 0-934070-19-9